OPINIONS OF THE WASHINGTON PRESS.

A compact, well made up, and neatly printed little volume ; just the thing for visitors at the Capital.—*The Evening Star.*

It is well gotten up, and every traveller should buy a copy. It is handsomely bound, and remarkably accurate. We bespeak for it a large sale.—*The Gazette.*

We have received a copy of Roose's Companion and Guide to Washington and Vicinity—a neat little well-bound book that can be conveniently carried in the pocket, and which contains a plain and handsome chart of the city and graphic pictorial and narrative descriptions of every place and object of interest in the District.—*The Daily Critic.*

"Roose's Companion and Guide to Washington and Vicinity" is an illustrated work of 140 pages, introducing at a glance objects of interest to the attention, and narrating facts connected with them. The compilers of the manual were evidently well acquainted with the subjects treated. The work is complete in itself, and one of the best guides to the national capital ever issued. Every stranger should have one.—*Washington Chronicle.*

One of the most exquisite Companion and Guide Books of Washington and vicinity ever printed has just been published by Mr. W. S. Roose, the well-known cigar and tobacco merchant, of this city. In this excellent production Mr. Roose has exhibited that thoroughness and care which has characterized him in all his enterprises in this city. The thousands of visitors who are coming to the capital of the nation from all sections of the country will find this book of incalculable value as a guide and companion in their tours of inspection. Everything of interest in the city and vicinity can be found in its ample pages. It introduces at a glance all objects of interest to the attention, and then narrates facts connected with them; in other words, it answers all questions which would naturally arise in an appreciative mind relative to what is presented to the view. It gives a history of the District of Columbia, and a correct and comprehensive plan of the city. It also gives a large number of elegant engravings illustrative of the most prominent buildings, statuary, and interesting historical features of the Federal Capital. Descriptions of everything of interest in the Capital are given in the minutest detail, as well as everything of importance in the various public buildings. Arlington, Mount Vernon, Soldiers' Home, and Rock Creek are all completely and with scrupulous accuracy set forth for the instruction and profit of our Centennial visitors. The compiler of the manual has the reputation of being well acquainted with the subjects treated of, and the work is destined to meet with the favor and appreciation of all who may visit our magnificent city. —*National Republican.*

THE various guide-books hitherto published descriptive of the numerous places and scenes of interest at the capital of the United States have been either too cumbrous or lamentably incomplete. The want of one which should be at the same time comprehensive and portable has been greatly felt during the present summer, when the overflow of visitors to the Centennial, spending a day or two seeing Washington, amounts to so considerable a number. Such a want has been supplied by our enterprising fellow-townsman Mr. W. S. Roose, who in a neat form has published a small volume, which, as the old saying has it, is as full of well-stated matter as "an egg is of meat." It commences with a brief history of the District, with a plan of the city, after which each place of interest is described in a concise and comprehensive manner, interspersed with numerous elegant engravings. In fact, an utter stranger in the city could, with the help of this valuable volume, find his way about, and see more in one day than one without it could in a week. In addition to the description of the public buildings and private institutions it also contains a complete record of all the hotels, churches, places of amusement, markets, railroads, horse-cars, schools; contains, in fact, everything a stranger or the natives want to know. The compiler of the manual is one of our most popular and enterprising merchants, who has the reputation of being thoroughly acquainted with the subjects presented, and who is, besides, a man of excellent business qualifications. He comprehended just what was wanted by the people, and set himself to work to produce it, with what success can be readily seen by the large sales which have already been made by our newsdealers. Our Centennial visitors have already voted Mr. Roose a friend indeed, while the Guide is so desirable that no resident of Washington but will find it useful, interesting, and suggestive.—*The Sunday Herald.*

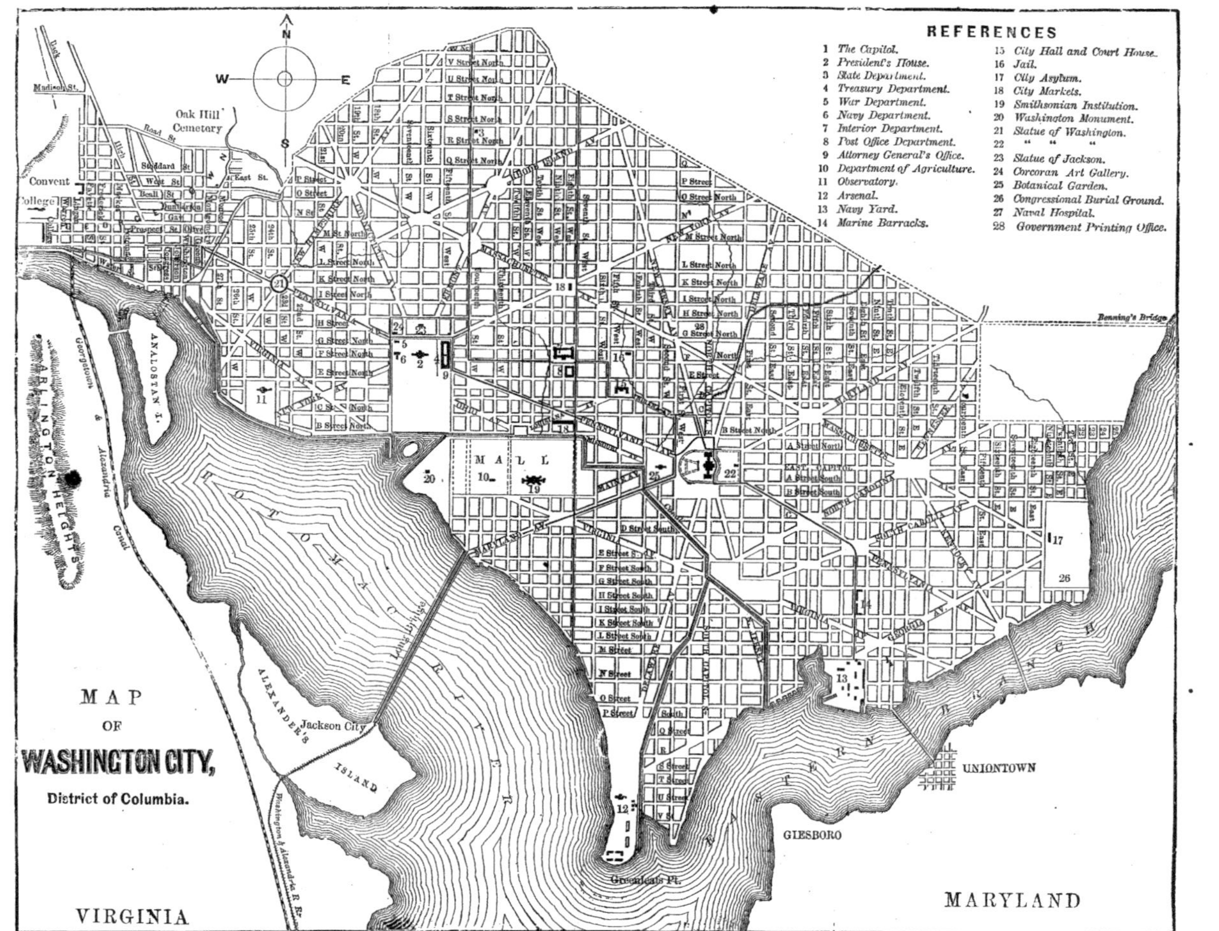
MAP
OF
WASHINGTON CITY,
District of Columbia.
REFERENCES
1 The Capitol.
2 President's House.
3 State Department.
4 Treasury Department.
5 War Department.
6 Navy Department.
7 Interior Department.
8 Post Office Department.
9 Attorney General's Office.
10 Department of Agriculture.
11 Observatory.
12 Arsenal.
13 Navy Yard.
14 Marine Barracks.
15 City Hall and Court House.
16 Jail.
17 City Asylum.
18 City Markets.
19 Smithsonian Institution.
20 Washington Monument.
21 Statue of Washington.
22 " " "
23 Statue of Jackson.
24 Corcoran Art Gallery.
25 Botanical Garden.
26 Congressional Burial Ground.
27 Naval Hospital.
28 Government Printing Office.
N
S
E
W
Oak Hill Cemetery
Convent
College
ANALOSTAN I.
ARLINGTON HEIGHTS
Georgetown & Alexandria Canal
ALEXANDER'S ISLAND
Jackson City
Washington & Alexandria R. R.
Long Bridge
POTOMAC RIVER
EASTERN BRANCH
MALL
Greenleafs Pt.
GIESBORO
UNIONTOWN
Benning's Bridge
VIRGINIA
MARYLAND

ROOSE'S

Companion and Guide

TO

WASHINGTON

AND

VICINITY.

Third Edition.

GIBSON BROTHERS, PRINTERS.
1876.

PUBLISHERS' PREFACE.

It is hoped this little book will prove a pleasant as well as useful Guide to the visitor to the Federal city.

Its purpose is to introduce at a glance objects of interest to the attention, and then narrate facts connected with them; in other words, to answer the questions which would naturally arise in an appreciative mind relative to what is presented to the view.

The compiler of the manual has the reputation of being well acquainted with the subjects treated of; and we shall be disappointed if the work does not fully equal what could reasonably be expected.

CONTENTS.

ILLUSTRATIONS.

The Capitol, (East Front.)

THE DISTRICT OF COLUMBIA.

NO American citizen should remain contentedly ignorant of the history of the District of Columbia, and of the events which led to its selection for the permanent seat of the Federal Government.

The Continental Congress opened its first session in Philadelphia, Pa., Sept. 5, 1774, and the succeeding year it also met in that city. For several seasons the fortune of war caused its migration from place to place. In Dec. 20, 1776, it met in Baltimore; but again, March 4, 1777, it met in Philadelphia. In Sept. 27, 1777, it convened at Lancaster, Pa., and Sept. 30, 1777, at York, Pa. July 2, 1778, it returned to Philadelphia, where it continued to meet until 1783, when it was expelled by a mob, which the State authorities did not suppress. Congress then adjourned to Princeton, N. J., June 30, 1783. Nov. 26, 1783, it met at Annapolis, Md.; and it was while in session here that Gen. Washington, Dec. 23, resigned his commission as general-in-chief of the army at the close of the revolutionary contest. Nov. 1, 1784, it met at Trenton, N. J., from which it adjourned to meet Jan. 11, 1785, in New York city. This last continued its place of meeting until the adoption of the Constitution of the United States, in 1788.

It was in the city of New York the First Federal Congress assembled—and the electoral votes were counted for the election of the first President of the United States. Gen. Washington was inaugurated President on the balcony of Federal Hall, (the site of the present New York Custom-house,) April 30, 1789.

The question "where the permanent seat of government should be located" gave rise to anxious debates even in the Continental Congress; and in the Convention which framed the Constitution the subject was waived because graver issues demanded the attention of that body, and it was deemed hazardous to decide upon what necessarily involved great local irritation.

The question, however, early engaged the attention of the First Federal Congress. Pennsylvania was anxious to have again within her territory the seat of power. New York was determined to retain, if she could, the possession which she held. New Jersey, Delaware, Maryland, and Virginia, each stretched out an eager hand, presenting a several plea, for the coveted prize. The New England States seem to have kept silent as regarded their own claims, while the extreme Southern States, supported by Maryland and Virginia, determined to have the capital brought further South than either New York or Philadelphia. The South Carolinians were particularly anxious Philadelphia should not be selected because of the Quakers, who "were continually dogging Southern members with their schemes of emancipation." Not only were newspapers filled with the discussion of the question, but private journals and the correspondence of the period teem with the controversy.

At length a bill passed the House, Sept. 22, 1789, ayes 31, noes 17, locating the permanent capital "on the river Susquehanna, in the State of Pennsylvania." This location was bitterly opposed by Mr. Madison, who led the Southern members, and who was supposed also to express the wishes of President Washington. In the Senate the bill was amended: the "Delaware river" and the neighborhood of Philadelphia, "including Germantown," was substituted instead, and some other new provisions were inserted. On the return of the bill to the House it was again strenuously opposed by Mr. Madison, who at last succeeded in having an unimportant amendment introduced, hoping that the delay consequent upon its consideration in the Senate would cause its being laid over to the next session of Congress. In this desire he was gratified. Instead of passing the bill the Senate "postponed" its consideration, and Congress adjourned the next day, Sept. 29, 1789.

At the next session of Congress the vexed question was again introduced. Partisanship ran high, and, in the opinion of many, upon its disposition seemed to hang the continued existence of the recently-formed Union. It was at this juncture that another question, involving the finances of the Republic, about which great diversity of opinion prevailed, and which also had enlisted warm and excited feeling, was made the basis of a compromise between the contending parties.

Alexander Hamilton, of New York, Secretary of the Treasury, had proposed the assumption by the Federal Government of the State debts. This was strongly opposed by Virginia and the Southern States. It was ascertained that it required the change of two votes to carry into effect the financial project. To accomplish this, and also settle the question of the selection of a place for the permanent capital, the aid of Thomas Jefferson, then recently returned from France, and appointed Secretary of State, was invoked.

The great democrat proposed that the subject should be talked over at a dinner, to which Hamilton was invited. It was there settled that if the votes of Lee and White, of Virginia, should be changed in favor of assumption, that Hamilton and Robert Morris, of Pennsylvania, would bring such an influence to bear upon the question of the location of the capital as would insure its permanent establishment upon the banks of the Potomac.

The bargain was faithfully kept. Hamilton's financial scheme was adopted, and on the 31st May, 1790, Pierce Butler, of South

Carolina, obtained permission of the Senate "to bring in a bill to determine the permanent seat of Government of the United States."

The bill located a district of territory for this purpose not exceeding ten miles square, "on the river Potomac, at some space between the mouths of the Eastern Branch and Conogocheague;" the capital to be removed thither in 1800, and until that time the temporary capital was to be established in Philadelphia. It passed the Senate July 1, 1780, ayes 14, noes 12. Four attempts were made in the House to change the site of the Federal District, but were voted down, and the Senate bill was finally agreed to, July 9, 1790, by a vote of 32 ayes to 29 noes. It received the signature of the President July 16, 1790.

[Maryland, by an act passed Dec. 28, 1788, and Virginia, by an act of Dec. 3, 1789, had previously authorized the cession of such portions of their territory as might be selected by Federal authority for the seat of the General Government.]

An amendatory act, which passed Congress March 3, 1791, repealed so much of the act of July 16, 1790, as required the whole District to be located above the mouth of the Eastern Branch, and authorized the President "to make any part of the said territory below the said limit, and above the mouth of Hunting creek, a part of the said District, so as to include a convenient part of the Eastern Branch, and of the lands lying on the lower side thereof, and also the town of Alexandria." It was provided that no public buildings should be erected otherwise than on the Maryland side of the Potomac.

A proclamation had been issued by President Washington, dated Philadelphia, Jan. 24, 1791, defining the boundaries of the District selected by him pursuant to the provisions of the first act. This was now followed by another proclamation amendatory of the other, dated Georgetown, March 30, 1791. The boundaries of the territory were therein declared to be as follows:

"Beginning at Jones' Point, being the upper cape of Hunting creek, in Virginia, and at an angle in the outset of 45 degrees west of the north, and running in a direct line ten miles for the first line; then beginning again at the same Jones' Point, and running another direct line at a right angle with the first, across the Potomac, ten miles, for the second line; then from the terminations of the said first and second line, running two other direct lines, of ten miles each, the one crossing the Eastern Branch aforesaid and the other the Potomac, and meeting each other in a point." * * * "And the territory so to be located, defined, and limited shall be the whole territory accepted by the said act of Congress as the District for the permanent seat of the Government of the United States."

This territory contained a surface of *ten miles square*, forming an area of 100 square miles, or 64,000 acres, and included both margins of the Potomac. Its situation lay between 38° 48′ and 38° 59′ north latitude. The Capitol, afterward erected near its centre, is in 76° 55′ 30.54″ west longitude from Greenwich. Georgetown and Alexandria were within its limits—the remainder was plantation or farm land.

President Washington appointed, Jan., 1791, ex-Governor Thomas Johnson, of Md., Dr. David Stuart, of Va., and the Hon. Daniel Carroll, of Rock Creek, Md., the first three Commissioners pursuant to the provisions of the act of July 16, 1790, who were empowered "to survey" and "define and limit a district of territory * * for the permanent seat of Government." They were also "to have power to purchase or accept such quantity of land on the eastern side of the said river, [Potomac,] within the said district, as the President shall deem proper for the use of the United States," and "provide suitable buildings for the accommodation of Congress and of the President, and for the public offices of the Government of the United States;" all subject to the approval of the President.*

Interesting as the history really is of the work accomplished by the Commissioners, their vexatious trials and various disappointments, the limited space of the present publication will only permit a recapitulation of the main results of their efforts.

The bargain and purchase of the land occupied by the Federal City from the original proprietors was brought about by the following arrangement:

Extracts from the Agreement of the Nineteen Original Proprietors.

The limits of the District of Columbia, as they now exist, having been fixed and proclaimed in March, 1791, under the authority of acts of Congress, *nineteen* of the principal proprietors of the lands constituting the present site of the city of Washington drew up and signed a general agreement among themselves, dated March 30, 1791, which they presented to the Commissioners, as the basis of the terms on which they should dedicate their lands to the purposes of the Federal City, and as such it was accepted by the Commissioners, and recorded in their books, on the 12th April, 1791, as follows:

"We, the subscribers, in consideration of the great benefits we expect to derive from having the Federal City laid off upon our lands, do hereby agree and bind ourselves, heirs, executors, and administrators, to convey, in trust, to the President of the United States, or Commissioners, or such person or persons as he shall appoint, by good and sufficient deeds, in fee simple, the whole of our respective lands which he may think proper to in-

---

* *Vide* Wyeth's Federal City. The compiler of this work has made very liberal use of Mr. Wyeth's book throughout, with the consent of that gentleman.

clude within the lines of the Federal City, for the purposes and on the conditions following:

"The President shall have the sole power of directing the Federal City to be laid off in what manner he pleases.

"He may retain any number of squares he may think proper for public improvements, or *other public uses;* and the lots only, which shall be laid off, shall be a *joint property* between the trustees on behalf of the public and each present proprietor; and the same shall be fairly and equally divided between the public and the individuals, as soon as may be, the city shall be laid off.

"For the *streets* the proprietors shall receive no compensation —but for the squares or lands in any form which shall be taken for public buildings, or *any kind* of public improvements or *uses*, the proprietors, whose lands shall be taken, shall receive at the rate of 25 pounds per acre, [sixty-six and two-thirds dollars,] to be paid by the public."

The lands were conveyed, in trust, by the original proprietors, to Thomas Beall, son of George, and John Mackall Gantt, to be by them disposed of, to be laid out as a Federal City, according to the above provisions.

In 1846 that portion of the District of Columbia which had been originally a portion of Virginia was retroceded by act of Congress back again to that State.

PLAN OF THE CITY.

A Frenchman, Major L'Enfant, originated the plan of the Federal City. He was a young officer belonging to the engineer corps of the French army, which aided us in our Revolutionary struggle. He early became a favorite of Gen. Washington, who approved his plan, and time has since confirmed the wisdom of that approval.

The Capitol was to be considered the centre of the city; from it the streets are counted north, south, east, and west; several of the avenues also radiate from it. The streets cross each other at right angles. Those running east and west are called after the letters of the alphabet, A, B, C, D streets, etc.; those running north and south, First, Second, Third streets, etc.

The avenues, named after the different States at the time the city was laid out—and a few others since added—cross these streets diagonally, and point in every conceivable direction.

North, South, and East Capitol streets intersect each other at the centre of the Capitol, and with an imaginary line continued west, divide the city into four sections. So there is a First street east and a First street west; an A street north and an A street south, and so on throughout.

There is no West Capitol street. Where that would have opened are gardens, etc., continued on until the grounds of the Smithsonian Institution are reached. Then succeed those surrounding the Agricultural Bureau building, and beyond them are those upon which the Washington Monument is erected. These *reservations* were intended to become an ornamented park, and

The Capitol, 1827.

Contemplated Monument to Lincoln, East Capitol Park.

in the early history of the city this space is called the **The Mall.** The grounds stretching south from the President's House connect with those surrounding the Monument.

The population of Washington City in 1810 was 8,208 ; in 1820, 13,247 ; in 1830, 18,826 ; in 1840, 23,364 ; in 1850, 40,001 ; in 1860, 61,122, and in 1870, 109,199.

THE CAPITOL.

THE United States Capitol, like the Capitol of ancient Rome, stands upon a hill, commanding a view westward, pronounced by the great traveller Humboldt one of the most beautiful his eyes had ever seen.

The plateau east extends an elevated plain for a considerable distance towards the banks of the Anacostia or Eastern Branch of the Potomac. The descents of the hill north and south are graduated admirably—art as well as nature assisting in producing the present graceful declivities.

The Capitol extends 751 feet 4 inches in length; the greatest breadth, including the steps of the Extensions, is 324 feet. The whole covers an area of three-and-a-half acres, or 153,112 square feet. Its cost to the present time has been a little under $13,000,000.

The centre portion of the building—the original Capitol—is built of yellowish sandstone, painted white, procured from an island in Acquia creek, Virginia. The island was purchased by Government from the Brent family, for $6,000, in 1791.

The Extensions are of white marble, slightly tinged with blue, obtained from Lee, Massachusetts. The monolith marble columns of the Extensions, of which there are one hundred, were taken from a quarry in Maryland.

The Dome is of iron, painted white, surmounted by the statue of Freedom, a bronze figure 19½ feet in height. The tip of the feather of this statue is 287 feet 11 inches above the base line of the building east. Capitol hill is within a fraction of 90 feet high; consequently the head of the statue is 377 feet above tide-water. In comparison, it may be interesting to say that the height of St. Peter's, at Rome, is stated in Knight's Cyclopædia to be, from the pavement to the top of the cross, 430 feet, and that of St. Paul's, at London, 404 feet.

The east Capitol park, stretching to the line of First st. east, has a frontage from B st. n. e. to B st. s. e., comprising a distance of 1,500 feet. The grounds are laid out according to a plan designed by Fred. Law Olmstead, of New York city, whose admirable ornamentation of Central Park has given him well-deserved prominence in the line of civil engineer and landscape gardener.

East of the centre portico, fronting either side, is a magnificent fountain, the two costing from forty to fifty thousand dollars. Costly lamps are interspersed throughout the grounds, making, at night-time, when lighted, a scene resembling our idea of fairy-land.

The eastern front of the Capitol is, properly speaking, its main front. It consists of a central Portico, 160 feet wide, with a projection, including the steps, of 65 feet, ornamented with 24 pillars and 12 pilasters, crowned with a pediment of 80 feet span. The whole front of what was the original Capitol is 352 feet; to this has been added, on either side, a colonnaded corridor of 44 feet; to these are attached the Extensions—that of the Senate on the north, and that of the House on the south end.

Each Extension is adorned with a portico 142 feet 8 in. wide, with a pediment of 72 feet span; 22 columns and 12 pilasters of the Corinthian style ornament the Extension porticoes.

The north and south fronts of the Capitol are alike. They extend 239 feet, and have each a portico 120 feet front, with a projection of 10 feet 6 in., and an entablature supported by 10 columns.

The west front of the Capitol is that with which strangers ordinarily are most familiar. It consists also of three ornamented porticoes; the central one a colonnade 100 feet front, with ten columns, eight of which are coupled, and a corresponding number of pilasters. This portico communicates with the Library of Congress. Then to each of the Extensions is attached a portico similar in architectural details to the north and south porticoes, with a length of 105 feet, ornamented with 10 columns.

This front of the Capitol possesses the advantage of the addition of the height of the hill, the top of which it occupies. The grounds extend to First st. west, and connect with the Botanical Garden.

Mr. Olmstead's plan proposes that "on the western side a stone terrace is to take the place of the upper grassy terrace. This stone terrace will remove the impression of insecurity and give the building an appearance of greater stability. The terrace is to be crowned with a handsome balustrade. The main western portico will be approached by a grand stone stairway."

We will now return to the

EAST CENTRAL PORTICO OF THE CAPITOL.

Immediately opposite and facing this Portico is **Greenough's Statue of Washington.** It is of colossal size, and has an interesting history. It was ordered in 1832, to be placed in the centre of the Rotunda, over the tomb or vaulted chamber built for the reception of the remains of Washington two stories beneath. The statue was finished in 1840, and the artist received $20,000 while working on it. Two other bills in connection with it were paid him, amounting to $10,435.85. The expenses of transportation from Italy, its erection in the Rotunda, of its subsequent removals, and of the pedestal upon which it is placed, have absorbed at least $13,000 more.

The chair upon which the figure sits is ornamented with the acanthus leaf and lions' heads. A small figure of Columbus and another of an Indian chief lean against its back. On the pedestal is inscribed the deserved eulogy on Washington, pronounced by Governor Henry Lee: "*First in war—first in peace—first in the hearts of his countrymen.*"

Washington sits in majesty, a sort of Jupiter. His person is nude to the waist. In his left hand is a sheathed sword, and with his right he points towards heaven.

On the right side of the chair is a *basso-relievo* of Phœbus-Apollo driving the chariot of the sun around the world—thus representing, in pictured allegory, the rising sun, the crest of the national arms of the United States. On the left side of the chair is depicted the infant Hercules strangling the serpent, while Iphiclus, his feebler twin-brother, stretched on the ground, shrinks from the contest; illustrating the genii of North and South America. On the back of the chair is inscribed: "*Simulacrum istud ad magnum Libertatus exemplum, nec sine ipsa duraturum.* **Horatio Greenough,** *faciebat.*" This has been translated by a distinguished scholar into—

"This statue cast in Freedom's stately form,
And by her e'er upheld.
"Horatio Greenough, Sculptor."

We will now ascend the steps. Upon them the Presidents of the United States are inaugurated; over a hundred thousand people, occupying the eastern park, might witness the ceremony.

Above the south end of the steps, on an elevated block, stands a marble group by Signor Persico, called **The Discovery,** on which he worked five years. It consists of two figures: Columbus holding the globe in his hand triumphant, while beside him, wondering, almost terror-stricken, is a female figure, symbolizing the Indian race. The suit of armor worn by Columbus is said to be a faithful copy of one he actually wore. The group cost $24,000.

On the north side of the steps, occupying a similar elevation, is another marble group—the artist, Horatio Greenough—called **Civilization, or the Settlement of the Country.** It represents the American pioneer in conflict with the Indian; the fight is desperate; the wife of the frontier settler, with her babe, and a faithful dog, are the adjuncts. Greenough was at work eight years on this group, which cost $24,000.

TYMPANUM OF THE PORTICO.

Before we enter the Portico we will direct attention to a group of allegorical figures of colossal size, said to be the design of John Quincy Adams, executed by Signor Persico, and occupying the tympanum of the Portico—just over our heads.

The central figure is the Genius of America, crowned with a star, holding a shield; on it are the letters U. S. A. The shield rests on an altar, on which, within an oaken wreath, is inscribed, "July 4, 1776." At her feet sits an eagle. Behind her is a spear. Hope on her left rests on an anchor. America directs the attention of Hope to Justice, who has in her right hand the Constitution of the United States. This composition is wrought in sandstone, and cost $1,500.

Within niches on either side of the Bronze Door are statues, also the work of Signor Persico.

The one on the north side is **War.** The figure grasps in his right hand a sword, in the other, a shield. His costume is Roman, and his belt and tunic are ornamented with appropriate symbols.

Peace is a female figure of majestic beauty, with a gentle, winning smile, and in simple flowing robes. She holds a fruit-bearing olive branch in her hand. The cost of these two figures was $6,000 each.

Above the Bronze Door, sculptured in stone by Capellano, is a bust of Washington crowned by Fame and Peace.

THE ROGERS BRONZE DOOR.

This is the main central door of the Capitol, and on it is a pictured history of events connected with the life of Columbus and the discovery of America.

The door weighs 20,000 pounds; is 17 feet high and 9 feet wide; it is folding or double, and stands sunk back inside of a bronze casing, which projects about a foot forward from the leaves or valves. On this casing are four figures at the top and bottom, representing Asia, Africa, Europe, and America. A border, emblematic of conquest and navigation, runs along the casing between them.

The Door has eight Panels beside the semi-circular one at the top. In each Panel is a picture in *alto-relievo.*

It was designed by Randolph Rogers, an American, and modelled by him in Rome, in 1858; and was cast by F. Von Müller, at Munich, in 1861.

The story the door tells is the **History of Columbus** and the **Discovery of America.**

The Panel containing the earliest event in the life of the discoverer is the lowest one on the south side, and represents "Columbus undergoing an Examination before the Council of Salamanca."

The Panel above it contains "Columbus' Departure from the Convent of La Rabida," near Palos. He is just setting out to visit the Spanish Court.

The one above it is his "Audience at the Court of Ferdinand and Isabella."

The next Panel is the top one of this half of the door, and represents the "Starting of Columbus from Palos on his first voyage."

The transom Panel occupies the semi-circular sweep over the whole door. The extended picture here is the "First Landing of the Spaniards at San Salvador."

The top Panel on the other leaf of the door represents the "First Encounter of the Discoverers with the Natives." In it one of the sailors is seen bringing an Indian girl on his shoulders a prisoner. The transaction aroused the stern indignation of Columbus.

The Panel next below this one has in it "The Triumphal Entry of Columbus into Barcelona."

The Panel below this represents a very different scene, and is "Columbus in Chains."

In the next and last Panel is the "Death scene." Columbus lies in bed. The last rites of the Catholic Church have been administered; friends and attendants are around him; and a priest holds up a crucifix for him to kiss, and upon it bids him fix his dying eyes.

On the Door, on the sides and between the Panels, are sixteen small statues, set in niches, of eminent contemporaries of Columbus. Their names are marked on the Door, and beginning at the bottom, on the side from which we started in numbering the Panels, we find the figure in the lowest niche is **Perez**; then above him is **Cortez**, and again standing over him is **Ojeda.**

Vespucci occupies the next niche on the door.

Then, opposite in line across the door, standing in two niches, side by side, are **Mendoza** and **Alexander VI.**

Then below them stand **Isabella** and **Ferdinand,** King and Queen of Spain; beneath them stands the **Lady Beatrice de Bobadilla**; beside her is **Charles VIII**, King of France.

The first figure of the lowest pair on the door is **Henry VII**, of England; beside him, stands **John II**, King of Portugal.

Then, in the same line with them, across the Panel, is **Pinzon.**

Justice. Genius of America. Hope.

War.—(P. 14.)

Peace.—(P. 14.)

Clock.—(P. 27.)

Lincoln.—(P. 27.)

In the niche above Pinzon stands **B. Columbus**, the brother of the great navigator.

Then comes **Vasco Nunez de Balboa**, and in the niche above, again at the top of the Door, stands the figure of **Francisco Pizarro**, the conqueror of Peru.

Between the Panels and at top and bottom of the valves of the Door are ten projecting heads. Those between the Panels are historians who have written on Columbus' voyages from his own time down to the present day, ending with Irving and Prescott.

The two heads at the tops of the valves are female heads, while the two next the floor possess Indian characteristics.

Above, over the transom arch, looks down, over all, the serene grand head of **Columbus**. Beneath it, the **American Eagle** spreads out his widely extended wings.

Mr. Rogers received $8,000 for his models, and Mr. Von Müller was paid $17,000 in gold for casting the Door. To a large portion of this latter sum must be added the high premium on exchange which ruled during the war, the cost of storage and transportation, and the expense of the erection of the Door in the Capitol after its arrival. These items would, added together, far exceed $30,000 in currency.

We will now enter the

ROTUNDA.

This magnificent apartment occupies the centre of the Capitol. It is 97 feet in diameter and 300 feet in circumference. Its height, from the floor to the centre of the pictured canopy which overhangs it, is 180 feet 3 inches.

We will first look at the pictures which surround its circuit. There are eight of them, each occupying a large panel, and they measure 18 by 12 feet.

The first in point of event is the **Landing of Columbus** at

San Salvador in 1492; by John Vanderlyn; its cost was $12,000. This picture represents the scene Washington Irving so admirably describes in his "Voyages of Columbus," occurring the morning the boats brought the little Spanish band from the ships to the shore. "Columbus first threw himself upon his knees; then rising, drew his sword, displayed the royal standard, and, assembling round him the two captains, with Rodrigo de Escobeda, notary of the armament, Rodrigo Sanchez, [the royal inspector,] and the rest who had landed, he took solemn possession of the island in the name of the Castilian sovereigns." The picture contains the figures of Columbus, the two Pinzons, Escobedo, all bearing standards; Sanchez, inspector; Diego de Arana, with an old-fashioned arquebus on his shoulder; a cabin-boy kneeling; a mutineer in a suppliant attitude; a sailor in an attitude of veneration for Columbus; a soldier whose attention is diverted by the appearance of the natives, and a friar bearing a crucifix.

The second picture in succession of event, 1541, is **De Soto's Discovery of the Mississippi**, painted by Wm. H. Powell; cost $15,000. The scene is a view of the Mississippi river, with islands in sight and canoes filled with Indians. On the bank, soldiers and priests are planting a cross; to the left are wigwams and a group of Indians. De Soto on horseback is approaching the river in state, attended by a train of followers. A camp-chest, with arms, and a soldier dressing his wounded leg, are accessories of the painting.

The next in order of time, 1613, is **The Baptism of Pocahontas**, by John Gadsby Chapman; cost $10,000.

This picture tells its own story. The characters introduced are Pocahontas, John Rolfe, afterwards her husband, with the Rev. Alex. Whitaker, who is performing the ceremony; Sir Thomas Dale stands on his right, his standard-bearer and page near him. The sister of Pocahontas, with her child, is seated on the floor;

Opechankanough, an Indian chief, also is seated, while Nantaquaas and Opachisco, her brother and uncle, stand near her. Other figures, male and female, are stationed in different parts of the church; among them are Richard Wyffin, Mr. and Mrs. Forrest, John and Anne Laydon, and Henry Spilman.

The succeeding picture, in chronological series, is **The Embarcation of the Pilgrims** from Delft-Haven, in Holland, 21st July, 1620. Painted by Robert Walter Weir. Cost $10,000.

The scene depicted is the delivery of the parting prayer of Mr. Robinson, the pastor of the little congregation, on board the *Speedwell*, surrounded by the pilgrims and their friends. The persons represented are the pastor, then Elder Wm. Brewster, with open Bible before him, Mrs. Brewster and a sick child, Gov. Carver, Wm. Bradford, Mr. and Mrs. Fuller, Miles Standish and Rose, his wife, Mrs. Carver and child, Mrs. Bradford, Captain Reynolds and sailor, with several children, a nurse, etc.

The four other pictures were painted by Col. John Trumbull, son of Jonathan Trumbull, governor of Connecticut previous to and during the Revolution. Col. Trumbull was himself at one time aid-de-camp of General Washington, but retired from the service in 1777.

The Trumbull series of pictures are especially valuable, because each of the many faces painted in them are actual likenesses, for which many of the subjects sat to the artist, and when this was not the case, copies of portraits at the time in the possession of the respective families were introduced. The paintings are the result of many years' devotion to his art by Col. Trumbull, and of a patriotic endeavor to perpetuate the grand deeds which they commemorate.

Col. Trumbull received for these four pictures $32,000. They were ordered in 1817 and finished in 1824. Col. Trumbull was born 1756; died 1843.

The Declaration of Independence, 1776. The room is copied from that in which Congress sat. The Committee of Five who reported the draft of the Declaration, Jefferson, John Adams, Franklin, Sherman, and R. R. Livingston, stand near the table at which Hancock, the president, sits.

The other portraits are, commencing on the extreme left, 1, George Wythe, of Va.; 2, Wm. Whipple and, 3, Josiah Bartlett, of N. H.; 4, Benj. Harrison, of Va.; 5, Thomas Lynch, of S. C.; 6, Richard Henry Lee, of Va.; 7, Samuel Adams, of Mass.; 8, George Clinton, of N. Y.; 9, William Paca and, 10, Samuel Chase, of Md.; 11, Lewis Morris and, 12, William Floyd, of N. Y.; 13, Arthur Middleton and, 14, Thomas Hayward, of S. C.; 15, Charles Carroll, of Md.; 16, George Walton, of Ga.; 17, Robert Morris, 18, Thomas Willing, and, 19, Benjamin Rush, of Pa.; 20, Elbridge Gerry and, 21, Robert Treat Payne, of Mass.; 22, Abraham Clark, of N. J.; 23, Stephen Hopkins and, 24, William Ellery, of R. I.; 25, George Clymer, of Pa.; 26, William Hooper and, 27, Joseph Hewes, of N. C.; 28, James Wilson, of Pa., and 29, Francis Hopkinson, of N. J.

Then comes the Committee of Five, already noted; after which, still continuing, are—

35, Richard Stockton, of N. J.; 36, Francis Lewis, of N. Y.; 37, John Witherspoon, of N. J.; 38, Samuel Huntington, 39, William Williams, and, 40, Oliver Wolcott, of Conn.; 41, John Hancock, of Mass., President of Congress; 42, Charles Thompson, of Pa.; 43, George Reed and, 44, John Dickinson, of Del.; 45, Edward Rutledge, of S. C.; 46, Thomas McKean, of Pa.; and, 47, Philip Livingston, of N. Y.

Surrender of General Burgoyne, Saratoga, Oct. 17, 1777. "The painting represents Gen. Burgoyne, attended by Gen. Phillips, and followed by other officers, arriving near the marque of Gen. Gates.

"Gen. Gates has advanced a few steps to meet his prisoner, who, with Gen. Phillips, has dismounted, and is in the act of offering his sword, which Gen. Gates declines to receive, and invites them to enter and partake of refreshments. A number of the principal officers of the American army are assembled near their General." These we will now enumerate.

(The numbering commences on the extreme left of the picture.)

1, Major Lithgow, of Mass.; 2, Colonel Cilly and, 3, General Stark, of N. H.; 4, Captain Seymour, of Conn., of Sheldon's horse; 5, Major Hull, and, 6, Colonel Greaton, of Mass.; 7, Major Dearborn, and, 8, Colonel Scammell, of N. H.; and, 9, Colonel Lewis, Quartermaster-General, N. Y. 10, Major-General Phillips, of the British army; 11, Lieutenant-General Burgoyne, British, and, 12, General Baron Reidesel, German. 13, Colonel Wilkinson, Deputy Adjutant-General, American; 14, General Gates; 15, Colonel Prescott, Mass. Volunteers; 16, Colonel Morgan, Va. Riflemen; 17, Brigadier-General Rufus Putnam, of Mass.; 18, Lieutenant-Colonel John Brooks, late Governor of Mass.; 19, Reverend Mr. Hitchcock, Chaplain, of R. I.; 20, Major Robert Troup, Aid-de-Camp, N. Y.; 21, Major Haskell, of Mass.; 22, Major Armstrong, Aid-de-Camp; 23, Major-General Philip Schuyler, Albany; 24, Brigadier-General Glover, of Mass.; 25, Brigadier-General Whipple, N. H. Militia; 26, Major Matthew Clarkson, Aid-de-Camp, N.Y., and, 27, Major Ebenezer Stevens, of Mass., Commander of Artillery.

Surrender of Lord Cornwallis, at Yorktown, Oct. 19, 1781. This was the triumphant closing scene of the war; and the glory of the triumph seems to linger on the glowing canvas.

"The painting represents the moment when the principal officers of the British army, conducted by Gen. Lincoln, are passing the two groups of American and French generals, and entering between the two lines of the victors."

The names of the officers represented will be found below. The portraits of the French officers were obtained in Paris in 1787, and were painted from the living men in the house of Mr. Jefferson, then Minister to France from the United States.

"Lord Cornwallis himself did not appear. The British forces were led by Gen. O'Hara, who, approaching Gen. Washington, took off his hat and apologized for the non-appearance of Lord Cornwallis, on account of indisposition. Washington received him with dignified courtesy, but pointed him to Major-General Lincoln as the officer who was to receive the submission of the garrison."

1, Count Deuxponts, Colonel of French Infantry; 2, Duke de Laval Montmorency, Colonel of French Infantry; 3, Count Custine, Colonel of French Infantry; 4, Duke de Lauzun, Colonel of French Cavalry; 5, General Choizy; 6, Viscount Viomenil; 7, Marquis de St. Simon; 8, Count Fersen, Aid-de-Camp; and, 9, Count Charles Damas, Aid-de-Camp of Count Rochambeau; 10, Marquis Chastellux; 11, Baron Viomenil; 12, Count de Barras, Admiral; 13, Count de Grasse, Admiral; 14, Count Rochambeau, General en Chef des Française; 15, General Lincoln; 16, Colonel Ebenezer Stevens, of the American Artillery; 17, General Washington, Commander-in-Chief; 18, Thomas Nelson, Governor of Va.; 19, Marquis La Fayette; 20, Baron Steuben; 21, Colonel Cobb, Aid-de-Camp to General Washington; 22, Colonel Trumbull, Secretary to General Washington; 23, Major-General James Clinton, N. Y.; 24, General Gist, Maryland; 25, General Anthony Wayne, Penn.; 26, General Hand, Adjutant-General, Penn.; 27, General Peter Muhlenberg, Penn.; 28, Major-General Henry Knox, Commander of Artillery; 29, Lieutenant-Colonel E. Huntington, Acting Aid-de-Camp of General Lincoln; 30, Colonel Timothy Pickering, Quartermaster-General; 31, Colonel Alexander Hamilton, Commanding Light

Infantry; 32, Colonel John Laurens, of S. C.; 33, Colonel Walter Stuart, of Philadelphia; and, 34, Colonel Nicholas Fish, of N. Y.

Resignation of General Washington: Annapolis, Dec. 23, 1783. General Washington, after taking leave of his old comrades at New York, accompanied by only two of them, proceeded to Annapolis, where Congress was then sitting, and there resigned his commission.

The persons introduced, whose portraits are given, are:

1, Thomas Mifflin, of Pa., President of Congress; 2, Charles Thompson, of Pa; 3, Elbridge Gerry, of Mass.; 4. Hugh Williamson, of N. C.; 5, Samuel Osgood, of Mass.; 6, Edward McComb, of Del.; 7, George Partridge, of Mass.; 8, Edward Lloyd, of Md.; 9, R. D. Spaight and 10, Benjamin Hawkins, of N. C.; 11, A. Foster, of N. H.; 12, Thomas Jefferson, of Va.; 13, Arthur Lee, of Va.; 14, David Howell, of R. I.; 15, James Monroe, of Va.; 16, Jacob Reid, of S. C., members of Congress; 17, James Madison, of Va., spectator; 18, William Ellery, of R. I.; 19, Jeremiah Townley Chase, of Md.; 20, S. Hardy, of Va.; 21, Charles Morris, of Pa., members; 22, General George Washington; 23, Colonel Benjamin Walker, and 24, Colonel David Humphrys, Aids-de-Camp; then, 25, General Smallwood, of Md.; 26, General Otho Holland Williams, of Md.; 27, Colonel Samuel Smith, of Md.; 28, Colonel John E. Howard, of Baltimore, Md.; 29, Charles Carroll, and two daughters, of Md.; 30, Daniel, of St. Thomas Jennifer, Md.; 31, Mrs. Washington, and her grandchildren, spectators.

Relievos in the Rotunda.

Over each of the four doors leading from the Rotunda are *alto-relievos* in stone. The cost of the four is said to have been $14,000.

The group over the east door is "The Landing of the Pilgrims on Plymouth Rock in 1620." The artist was Signor Enrico Causici, of Verona, a pupil of Canova.

That over the north doorway is "William Penn's Treaty with the Indians in 1686." A Frenchman, Monsieur N. Gevelot, executed this work in 1827.

Over the door opening west is "The Preservation of Captain Smith by Pocahontas in 1606." Signor Capellano, another pupil of Canova, was the artist. It was executed in 1825.

The group over the doorway leading south is the "Conflict between Daniel Boone and the Indians, 1775." This is the work of Causici.

Eight long narrow *basso-relievos* of arabesque pattern are in the panels above the pictures. Four of them contain medallion heads. The heads are portraits of **Columbus, Cabot, Sir Walter Raleigh, and La Salle.** The whole of them cost $9,500.

There is above the architrave a sunken space, now a blank wall, nine feet high, surrounding the chamber. It is proposed that this recessed panel shall be filled with a picture or an *alto-relievo*, illustrative of "American History," appearing a procession of figures making the rise from aboriginal barbarism to our present civilization.

A short distance above the frieze thirty-six tall windows admit a flood of light into the chamber. Above them springs the arch of the dome, lessening in curvature like the inside of an egg-shell, until contracted to a space of 50 feet in diameter, forming the eye of the dome.

Beyond and over this open eye, within the canopy that overhangs it, is painted Brumidi's allegorical fresco of the Apotheosis of Washington.*

* The word "Apotheosis" is of Greek origin, and means the enrolment of a mortal among the gods.

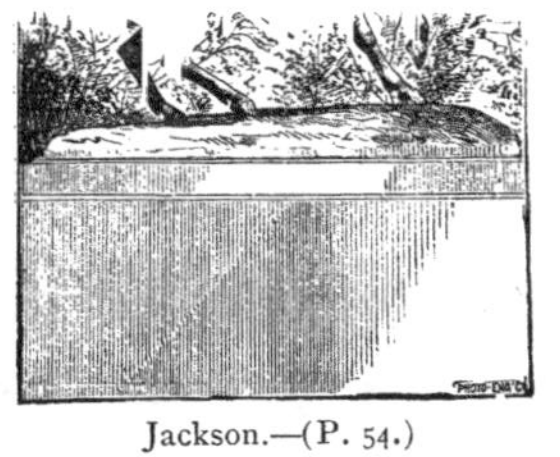

Jackson.—(P. 54.)

Washington.—(P. 46.)

Scott.—(P. 45,)

Freedom.—(P. 26.)

Greenough's Washington.—(P. 12.)

The Discovery.—(P. 13.)

Civilization.—(P. 14.)

Brumidi's Allegorical Painting.

The central group of the picture represents WASHINGTON seated in majesty. On his right is the GODDESS OF LIBERTY, and on his left is a winged idealization of VICTORY and FAME—sounding a trumpet and displaying the victor's palm. Before the three, forming a semicircle, are thirteen female figures. They represent the thirteen original States; each is crowned with a star; and they hold up a ribbon-banner inscribed "*E Pluribus Unum.*"

Below this centre group are six other groups round the base of the canopy.

The first, occupying the west, is WAR. FREEDOM, with uplifted sword, is striking down tyranny and kingly power. An angry EAGLE, striking with his beak, is fighting for, and by the side of, FREEDOM.

The second is AGRICULTURE. Ceres, Flora, and Pomona figure in this group.

Then succeeds MECHANICS. VULCAN, with his right foot resting on a cannon, and surrounded by machinery, forges, mortars, and cannon balls, is the stalwart genius of this group.

The next, and occupying the east, is COMMERCE. MERCURY holds in his hand a bag of gold, to which he is directing the attention of ROBERT MORRIS.

The group beside this symbolizes the MARINE. APHRODITE, [VENUS,] half risen from the waves, holds in her hand the Atlantic cable, given her by a winged cherub, and is about dropping it into the sea. NEPTUNE, astonished, is emerging from the deep.

The last is THE ARTS AND SCIENCES. MINERVA stands gloriously prominent with helmet and spear. Near her, attentive to her teachings, are BENJAMIN FRANKLIN, ROBERT FULTON, and S. F. B. MORSE. There are also boys, with wondering eyes and expressive gestures, listening to the instructions of a school-teacher.

This painting covers an area of 4,664 square feet. Mr. Brumidi received for his work $39,500.

The stairway still ascends above the picture, and traverses the top of the canopy between the two shells, until it reaches the "Tholus" or "lantern" of the Dome.

The Statue of Freedom

crowns the Dome. It weighs 14,985 pounds, and was placed in position Dec. 2, 1863. The forts then surrounding Washington fired a salute in honor of the occasion. Mr. Crawford received for his model $3,000, and the casting of it, by Mr. Clark Mills, with all the attending expenses, netted an additional sum of $20,796.82.

At night, the Rotunda, Dome, and Tholus are lighted by 1,280 gas-jets ignited by electricity. The electric-room is situated in the central portion of the building.

We will now descend from the Dome again to the Rotunda, and enter the doorway leading south from that apartment.

Passing through a small vestibule, we shall then find ourselves in the

Old Hall of Representatives.

This chamber, resembling an ancient Grecian theatre, is 95 feet long, and 60 feet in height to the most elevated point of the ceiling. Twenty-six pillars and pilasters of Potomac marble support a dome with painted caissons. A cupola, painted by Bonani, an Italian, admits light from above.

Under a sweeping arch near the dome is a colossal figure of LIBERTY, by Causici, in plaster. Beneath it, on the entablature, is sculptured, in stone, the American eagle in the act of taking wing, by Valperti, also an Italian.

Opposite, over the door through which we entered, stands the old marble clock of the Hall. It represents the Genius of History recording the events of the nation. She stands in a graceful attitude, with pen in hand, on a winged car rolling over a globe. The wheel of the car serves as the face of the clock. This beautiful work of art was executed by Signor C. Franzoni, an Italian, who died May 12, 1819. The credit of designing it is a matter of controversy.

This Old Hall is now used as a statuary-room, in compliance with a suggestion of Senator Justin S. Morrill, of Vermont, made when a member of the House, that "each State should be permitted to send the effigies of two of her chosen sons, in marble or bronze, to be placed permanently here." Other statuary, belonging to the Government, mostly of historical interest, with paintings, etc., have also been placed in their companionship.

Of this latter class we will first speak: Among them stands a plaster cast of

Houdon's Washington.

Houdon came from France with Franklin in 1785, and obtained his model from Washington himself. He remained a guest for two weeks at Mount Vernon. The present copy was taken by Hubard, and cost $2,000.

Bust of Kosciusko.

Born 1755, died 1817. The artist who made this bust was also a Pole, named Mochowski. He assumed as his American name that of Saunders. It cost $500.

Miss Ream's Statue of Lincoln.

In 1866 Congress appropriated $10,000 for a full-length statue of Mr. Lincoln. Miss Ream, of Washington city, received the commission for its execution. The work was finished in 1870, and on its completion an additional $5,000 was obtained by her from Congress.

Ames' Bust of Lincoln.

Mrs. Sarah Fisher Ames, of Mass., received an order in 1868 from Congress to make a bust of President Lincoln. She received $2,000 for her work. It stands on a Scotch granite pedestal, presented by A. Macdonald, Field & Co., of Aberdeen, Scotland.

Bust of Thomas Crawford.

Crawford was the artist who designed the statue of Freedom, the Senate Bronze Door, the marble group above it, and the marble figures ornamenting the tympanum of the Senate Extension Portico. His bust is the work of T. Gagliardi. The price paid for it was $100.

Statue of Alexander Hamilton.

Dr. Horatio Stone, of Washington city, executed this statue in Rome. It arrived from Italy in 1868, and cost $10,000.

The Bronze Statue of Thomas Jefferson,

by David d'Angers, a French sculptor, was presented to Congress by Lieutenant Uriah P. Levy, U. S. Navy, in 1834, but was not formally accepted by Government until 1873. It stood, long ago, in the Rotunda, and after its removal from there was placed in front of the President's House, a position it occupied for many years. After its acceptance, upon the motion of Senator Sumner it was finally located in the old Hall. This bronze was cast by *Honore Gonon et ses deux fils.*

The Portraits.

These are a Mosaic of Mr. Lincoln, presented by Signor Salviati, of Venice. Signor Salviati is the great manufacturer of mosaic work in Italy. The probable mercantile value of this mosaic is about $1,000. Also,

A full-length picture of Henry Clay, by Neagle. Cost $1,500.

A portrait of **Joshua R. Giddings**, by Miss C. L. Ransom. Cost, $1,000.

A likeness of **Charles Carroll**, of Carrollton, born 1737, died 1832; the last surviving signer of the Declaration of Independence. Painted by Chester Harding. Cost, $500.

In 1872 a portrait of **Gunning Bedford**, a member of the Continental Congress from Delaware, was presented by the heirs of the family to Government.

A portrait of **Thomas Jefferson**, by Sully—an original, esteemed an admirable picture—placed here in 1875. Cost, $200.

A portrait of **Benjamin West**, painted by himself, is also a recent addition.

An original portrait of **General Washington**, by Stuart, purchased in 1876, by the Joint Committee on the Library, from ex-Senator Chesnut, of Camden, S. C., for $1,200.

Statuary Furnished by the States.

Rhode Island contributed the first of all the States the permitted quota, viz:

Major-General Nathaniel Greene,

born 1742, died 1786. The sculptor was Henry K. Brown. The work is dated Rome, 1869, Aug. 6. And

Roger Williams,

the pioneer-apostle of liberty of religious opinion; born 1606, died 1683. The artist was Franklin Simmons, of R. I. The marble was cut in Rome. Date, 1870.

Connecticut was the next to send her marble representation. One is

Jonathan Trumbull,

the last colonial governor of the State, who became a tower of strength to the revolutionary movement. Born 1710; died 1785.

He was the father of the painter, Col. Trumbull; he also was the intimate friend of Washington, and because of their familiar intercourse Washington applied to him the soubriquet of *Brother Jonathan*. The other is

Roger Sherman,

the shoemaker, afterward lawyer, judge, delegate to Congress, one of the Committee of Five, and signer of the Declaration of Independence, is the other. Born 1721; died 1793. The artist, E. E. Ives, a native of Connecticut, made both these statues in Rome. They were formally unveiled February, 1872.

New York has sent in bronze

George Clinton,

who died at Washington city in 1812. Vice-President U. S. Artist, Henry R. Brown; 1873. Founders, Robert Wood & Co., Philadelphia. And

Robert R. Livingston,

one of the Committee of Five who presented the Report, but who was not a signer of the Declaration of Independence. He was the first chancellor of the State of New York, and administered the oath of office to President Washington. He was also Minister to France when the purchase of Louisiana was completed. E. D. Palmer, artist; 1874. Cast by F. Barbedienne, founder, Paris.

Gov. John Winthrop

is a contribution from the State of Massachusetts. By Richard S. Greenough, the brother of Horatio Greenough. And

Samuel Adams,

who has been proudly denominated "The Father of the Revolution." George Clymer wrote of him in 1773: "All good men should erect a statue to him in their hearts." Samuel Adams was born in Boston, Sept. 22, 1722; died Oct. 2, 1803. He was a cousin of John Adams, second President of the United States.

The bitterness of Tory hate against him is manifested in the words of Bernard, who wrote: "Damn Samuel Adams! every dip of his pen stings like a horned snake."

The artist, Miss Whitney, has produced an admirable statue of the Revolutionary hero.

Col. Ethan Allen

is one of the representative figures sent from Vermont. It is of colossal size. Artist, Lukin G. Mead.

Col. Edward D Baker.

This statue was ordered by Congress, and cost $10,000. Born in England, of poor parents, Col. Baker came a boy to this country, where, with his father, he worked at weaving. He eventually became a Senator of the U. S. from Oregon, and died at Ball's Bluff, near Leesburg, gallantly fighting rebellion at the head of his regiment, Oct. 21, 1861. The artist was Horatio Stone, and this statue was the last work of his graceful chisel. Doctor Stone died in Italy in 1875.

Passing out of the Old Hall through the south door we enter the House Extension of the Capitol.

The New Hall of Representatives

is in the centre of that Extension. The chamber is 139 feet long, 93 feet wide, and 36 feet high. It has a gallery on its four sides capable of having crowded into it 1,200 persons. Portions are allotted to the diplomatic corps and reporters of the press. There are also divisions for the families of the Cabinet officers, Senators, and Representatives; the remainder is for visitors.

The ceiling is of iron, gilded and bronzed, and is supported by trusses from the roof. Its centre is a skylight, panelled with glass; in each panel is painted the arms of a State.

Seats for the members, with desks in front of them, are ranged in successive semicircles facing the Speaker's desk. In front of it sit the various clerks and phonographic reporters.

A full length likeness of Washington, by Vanderlyn, which cost $2,500, is on one side of the Speaker's chair, and on the other side is a likeness of Gen. Lafayette, by Ary Scheffer, which was presented to Congress by the artist about 1824–'25.

A fresco by Brumidi, representing "Gen. Washington refusing Lord Cornwallis' request for an armistice at Yorktown, just before the final surrender," occupies a portion of the wall west of the portrait of Lafayette.

Corridors, paved with encaustic tiles, surround the Hall, and afford entrance to various rooms for the officers of the House and for the use of committees. The Speaker's room is a very elegant apartment south of the Hall.

Staircases of Tennessee marble on the east and west sides of the Hall lead to the galleries.

On the wall, above the western staircase, is Leutze's picture of "Western Emigration." Cost $20,000.

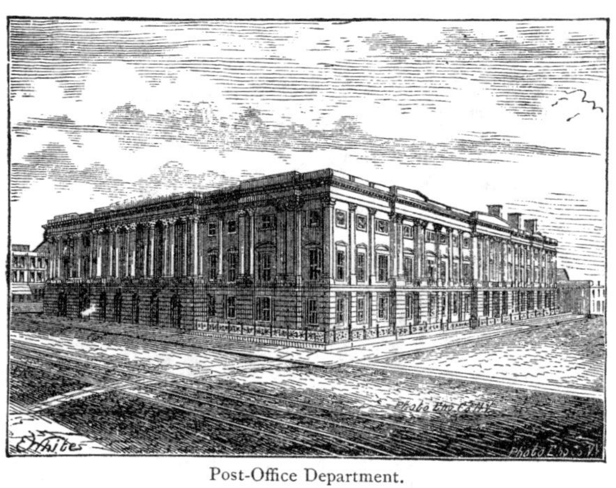

Post-Office Department.

Pennsylvania Avenue, from the Treasury to the Capitol.

Botanical Garden.

At the foot of this staircase is a bust, in bronze, of a Chippewa Indian chief, "The Buffalo."

An equestrian picture, on canvas, of Gen. Scott occupies the same position above the eastern staircase. It is still the property of the artist, Edward Troye.

At the foot of this staircase stands a statue of Thomas Jefferson, by Powers; it cost $10,000.

Various committee-rooms and rooms appropriated to newspaper reporters are situated in the upper story of the Extension, to which we now ascend.

There is also from here access to the Library of the House, which occupies the story above the communicating corridor leading from the Old Hall.

Above the roof of the Hall is the illuminating vault of the House. Hundreds of gas-jets are placed above the pictured skylight. They communicate with the electric apparatus by which the Rotunda and Dome is lighted, and at night flood the chamber with a brighter light than that of day.

We will now descend to the ground-floor. This is occupied by committee-rooms, closets, bath and store-rooms, the folding-room, House Restaurant, etc., etc.

Of the committee-rooms the most beautiful in wall ornamentation is that of the Committee on Agriculture. It is south of the west staircase. The frescoes illustrate subjects connected with agriculture. The artist was Signor Brumidi.

The central hall of the floor of this extension is lined with *scaglioni* and adorned with monolith marble columns of great beauty.

Beneath this story is the heating and ventilating apparatus of the House. The engineer in charge will explain the manner in which cool and hot air is forced into the Hall.

The Crypt.

Beneath the Rotunda is the CRYPT, so called from its resemblance to the chambers of that name in cathedrals. It has numerous pillars, supporting groined arches, and is dimly lighted.

There is here a huge marble figure—THE DYING TECUMSEH—the work of an Italian. It is not owned by Government.

A bust of PULASKI, by Mochowski, is also here, which it is hoped Government will eventually purchase.

The Tomb of Washington.

Beneath the Crypt is a vaulted chamber, built to receive the remains of Gen. Washington and his wife. Visitors, upon application to the police of the Capitol, will be shown what is called the Tomb.

Congress, in 1832, the centennial year of Washington's birth, made application to the then owner of Mount Vernon to obtain the remains of the illustrious dead, to be placed here, but they were refused; the chamber, consequently, has since remained empty.

Court of Claims.

On the ground floor of the centre portion of the Capitol, on the west side, is situated a suite of rooms occupied by the Court of Claims.

The Library of Congress

occupies the western projection of the original Capitol, and access is obtained to it from the Rotunda by the west door.

These beautiful halls were designed by Thos. U. Walter. They are of iron, including shelves; the floors are laid with encaustic tiles; consequently all is fire-proof. The centre hall is

91 feet long, 34 feet wide, and 38 feet high. The side halls are 95 feet long and 29½ feet wide.

The Library of Congress originated in 1800, and from that time until 1814 the number of volumes comprised about 3,000. It was destroyed by the British in that year, when they set fire to the Capitol.

Mr. Jefferson's library, then considered one of the finest in the country, was purchased by Congress for $23,950 in 1815, and became the nucleus of a new collection, which, in 1851, comprised 55,000 volumes. Dec. 25 of that year, a fire, originating from timbers carelessly exposed to flues, consumed 35,000 volumes, besides works of art, coins, etc., etc.

The number of volumes in the Library in 1874 was 274,157 volumes and 50,000 pamphlets. Jan. 1, 1876, the number of volumes reported is 293,507, and 60,000 pamphlets.

Although designed especially for the use of Congress and Government officials, any visitor over sixteen years of age can obtain books to read, *only in the Library*, by filling one of the blanks to be found on the tables, and presenting it at the Librarian's desk.

On the ground-floor, underneath the Supreme Court-room, is the law branch of the Library. The vestibule to this apartment is famous for its ornamentation of corn-stalk columns, with capitals of opening ears of corn. This room was once occupied by the Supreme Court of the United States.

Supreme Court-Room of the United States.

This chamber is situated in what was the north wing of the original Capitol, and occupies the eastern side of that portion of the building. It was the old United States Senate Chamber. It is semi-circular, 75 feet long, 45 feet high, and its greatest width 45 feet. It is ornamented with columns of Potomac marble, and has a dome ceiling. Around the semicircular wall are brackets, on which are placed the busts of deceased Chief-Justices. The room is beautifully carpeted.

The rooms in its vicinity are appropriated to the officers and judges of the Supreme Court.

In the robing-room hangs a portrait of Chief-Justice Marshall, by Rembrandt Peale, a companion-picture to his Washington. This portrait was presented to Chief-Justice Chase by the bar of New York, and at his death was bequeathed by him to the Supreme Court of the United States.

Leaving the Supreme Court-room, we pass into the Senate Extension, in the centre of which is the

Senate Chamber.

In general arrangement and appearance this Chamber resembles the Hall of Representatives, though smaller. It is 112 feet long and 82 feet wide. The desks of the Senators are of highly polished mahogany. In the skylight are painted symbols of Progress, the Union, the Army, the Navy, and the Mechanical Arts.

Immediately north of the Senate Chamber are three rooms of great beauty; the most westerly one is

The President's Room.

Dimensions, 23 feet 2 inches by 21 feet 8 inches, with a canopied ceiling. The whole room is elaborately decorated in fresco and distemper. On the walls are the portraits of President Washington and his Cabinet. The ceiling is covered with allegorical illustrations of Religion, Liberty, Executive Power, and Legislative Authority, with portraits of Columbus, Americus Vespucius, Wm. Brewster, and Benj. Franklin. The floor is tiled, but in winter is covered with a rich carpet. In this room towards the close of a session of Congress the President affixes his signature to bills.

The Marble Room.

The walls of this room are of polished Tennessee marble and plate-glass. Four Corinthian columns of Italian marble support the ceiling. Its length is 38 feet 7 inches, 19½ feet high, and width 21 feet 8 inches. It is used as a retiring-room by the Senators.

The Vice-President's Room

is of the same size as the President's, but the walls are unadorned. It is beautifully furnished, and here is hung Rembrandt Peale's celebrated likeness of Washington, which adorned the old Senate Chamber, and cost, in 1832, $2,000. Vice-President Wilson died in this room October, 1875.

Ladies' Reception Room.

This is elaborate in ornamentation, and its purpose is to provide a place where ladies may obtain interviews with Senators. It is situated east of the three rooms last described, and next it is the room of the Sergeant-at-Arms of the Senate, and also

The Senate Post-Office.

This is admirably furnished for use. The ceiling was painted by Brumidi at a cost of $5,000. On it is represented History, Geography, Physics, and the Telegraph.

We will now enter the hall leading to the east Senate Extension Portico, and arrive at

The Crawford Bronze Door.

This door illustrates Revolutionary and Federal history, and cost for models $6,000; for casting $50,495.11. One valve is War and the other Peace.

At the top of the War valve is the "Battle of Bunker Hill and Death of Warren, 1775." The next panel is the "Battle of Monmouth and Rebuke of Gen. Charles Lee, the traitor, 1778."

Then, again, below is "Yorktown—the gallantry of Hamilton, 1781;" and at the bottom of the door is a Hessian soldier in death-struggle with an American.

At the foot of the Peace valve is an allegorical representation of the blessings of Peace. Then, above it, is the "Ovation to Washington at Trenton, 1789." Next above that, "The First Inauguration of President Washington, 1789;" and in the top panel is pictured "The Laying of the Corner-stone of the United States Capitol, September 3, 1793."

The door was cast at Chicopee, Mass., by James T. Ames.

Above the door is a group in marble of History and Justice.

The Senate Extension Portico,

of which this is the door, has over its centre, in detached figures, an illustration of the "Progress of American Civilization and the Decadence of the Indian Races."

The centre figure is America. On her right [south] stands a soldier; next him is Commerce—a merchant; then comes Youth—two boys; Education succeeds—a schoolmaster, with a boy pupil; next, a Mechanic, resting against a wheel; and then are an Anchor and a Wheat Sheaf, which fill the rapidly narrowing space of the pediment.

On the left [north] of America is a Pioneer settler chopping a tree; then a Hunter; next him sits an Indian chief; beside him is an Indian woman with a babe; and then, again, filling up the narrow space on this side, is an Indian grave. These figures were modelled by Crawford. He was paid for them, including the cost of Justice and History, $20,000. The additional cost for cutting amounted to $29,150.

We will now return to the interior of the Senate Extension, and traverse again the beautiful hall, adorned with pillars and lined with scaglioni marble, communicating with the Portico.

Opposite the Senate Post Office [south] is the room of the OFFICIAL REPORTERS OF THE SENATE. It is fitted up especially to aid the corps of gentlemen engaged in this work, and is also a very beautiful apartment.

At the foot of the east staircase of the Senate is a statue of **Franklin**, by Hiram Powers; cost $10,000.

On the wall hangs Powell's picture of the **Battle of Lake Erie**, September 10, 1813; cost $25,000.

Ascending the stairs, we find magnificent corridors, paved with encaustic tiles, surrounding three sides of the Senate galleries.

In this story, in a vestibule opposite the entrance to the ladies' gallery, hang two pictures by Thomas Moran, on canvas, of the **Canon of the Yellowstone** and the **Canon of the Colorado.** Each cost $10,000.

Il Penserosa.

A beautiful female figure in marble, purchased by the Joint Committee on the Library, by Mozier, cost $2,000, is also placed here.

Committee-rooms surround the various corridors.

The illuminating loft of the Senate Chamber is reached by a stairway continued above the west staircase of the Senate Extension. The "Wilson Patent Electric Gas-lighter," which consists in the application of the "spark," is in use. The illuminating process differs from that by which the Rotunda and House is lighted.

Over the west staircase of the Senate, which is of white marble, hangs the picture of **The Storming of Chapultepec**, by James Walker; cost $6,000. This picture was originally painted for a panel in the Committee-room of Military Affairs of the House, and doubtless will eventually be placed there.

At the foot of this staircase is a statue of **John Hancock**, by Dr. Stone; cost $5,500.

The rooms on the west side of the corridor on the main floor, which we have again reached, are appropriated to the clerks of the Senate.

Ground Floor of the Senate Extension.

This, like the same story of the House Extension, contains a Restaurant, Bath and Committee-rooms, etc., etc. The walls of the corridors on this side, however, are profusely decorated with paintings, viz., busts of distinguished Americans, flowers, fruits, and animals, besides frescoes of historical events, etc. It would require weeks of inspection to enable the visitor to attain anything like an intelligent appreciation of their variety and excellence.

The Room of the Committee on Naval Affairs is especially of surpassing beauty. It is literally covered, ceiling and walls, with pictures and figures relating to the marine.

The Room of the Committee on Military Affairs is also profusely decorated. The pictures are illustrative of military service, and several of the famous battles of the Revolution are painted on the walls. A visitor should not neglect, if possible, to see these two rooms.

Beneath this story is the heating and ventilating apparatus, by means of which the Senate is heated and cooled. To many this is a most interesting portion of the Capitol to visit, and strangers are invariably treated with politeness and their questions answered by the employés in charge.

The Capitol Police.

The Capitol police consists of a representative appointed from each State. The officers are a captain and lieutenants.

The duties are to preserve order within the Capitol and grounds, (including the Botanical Garden;) to protect the public

Emancipation.—(P. 47.)

Capitol, West Front.

Patent Office.

Young Men's Christian Association Building.

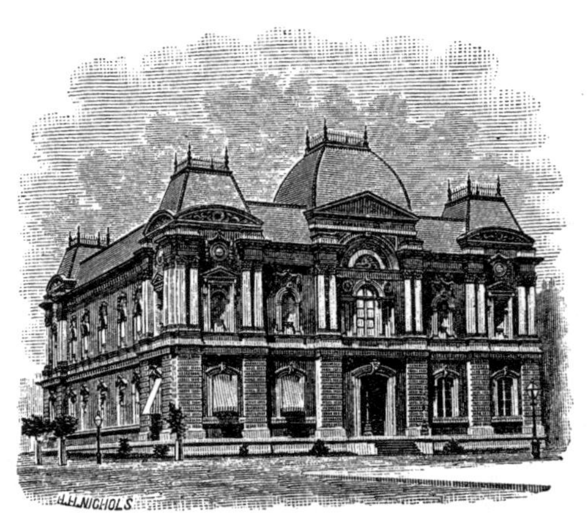

Corcoran Gallery of Art.

property from injury; enforce all prescribed rules; also to extend to visitors proper courtesies, and furnish them with all desired information.

They are on duty day and night, and because of their constant supervision ladies can, without fear of insult or molestation, wander at will anywhere throughout the building and grounds. Many of the gentlemen on this force have been distinguished soldiers in the late war.

History of the Building of the Capitol.

The corner-stone of the Capitol was laid with Masonic ceremonies September 18, 1793, by Master Mason George Washington, President of the United States.

The plan approved of was that of Doctor Wm. Thornton, born in the West Indies, an amateur civil engineer and draftsman. The practical architect first employed in its erection was Stephen Hallet, a Frenchman, who modified Thornton's plan and substituted some features of his own, which displeased Thornton, who possessed the ear of the President, and eventually became a commissioner. Hallet was dismissed. Hoban, the architect of the President's House, was then put in charge for a short period.

An Englishman, Mr. George Hadfield, was afterwards employed, and he, in conjunction with Hoban, succeeded in getting the north wing ready for occupation in 1800. The Senate, House of Representatives, Supreme Court, and Library were accommodated in the one wing.

Mr. Hadfield, however, became discontented and resigned his position. In 1803, Mr. Henry B. Latrobe, an Englishman of Huguenot descent, was his successor, and by him the south wing was completed. In 1814 the British burned out the two wings. The space now occupied by the Rotunda, up to that period, was only a wooden scaffolding, which united the two portions of the building.

Latrobe was employed to rebuild the wings, and also to design and erect the Rotunda and Dome. Becoming dissatisfied, he resigned in 1817. Mr. Charles Bulfinch, of Boston, an American, was his successor.

The foundation of the Rotunda was laid March 2, 1818. The Capitol, including the Rotunda and the first low-arched Dome, was considered finished in 1827. Mr. Bulfinch, after accomplishing his work, returned to Boston.

The corner-stone of the Extension was laid in 1851, July 4: Daniel Webster made the oration. Mr. Thomas U. Walter, of Pennsylvania, designed and erected the Extension (north and south) and the new Dome. The architect in charge in 1876 is Mr. Edward Clark, formerly a pupil of Mr. Walter. The cost of the Capitol to present date has been a little under $13,000,000.

The Botanical Garden,

under the efficient superintendence of Mr. Wm. R. Smith, is immediately west of the Capitol, lying between Maryland and Pennsylvania avenues. There is here a conservatory 300 feet long. There are ten smaller conservatories. The first buildings were erected in 1850. This portion of Reservation No. 2 was set apart for a Botanic Garden previous to the removal of the seat of Government to this city. It was, in 1850, a swamp, the chief source of ague around the Capitol. The tide ebbs and flows here in a large sewer covering a river known as the Tiber.

In the large conservatory note the majestic palms, in good variety, the graceful ferns, the formal succulents, in large assortment, with many botanical curiosities, viz: banana, mango, camphor, Caffre bread, India-rubber, sugar cane, dumb-cane of

South America, incense tree, bamboo, 20 varieties of passion flowers, coffee tree, cinnamon, black and betel peppers, and about 4,000 species and varieties of botanical interest.

RESERVATIONS.

There were originally set apart for various purposes seventeen reservations, designated in the early maps by figures from 1 to 17. Most of them still remain, with slight modifications, in possession of the Government. Their whole original area was 541 acres, 1 rood, 29 perches. Their present area is about 513 acres.

Res. 1—The President's Grounds.—This includes the surroundings of the Executive Mansion, extending from Lafayette Square on the north to the mouth of Tiber creek, in the neighborhood of the Washington Monument. On it are the Presidential Mansion, the Treasury, the War, Navy, and State Departments. 83 acres, 1 rood, 22 perches.

Res. 2—The Capitol Grounds.—This is the Mall, with the East and West Capitol Parks; its western line is 14th st. west. On it are the Capitol, the Botanical Garden, the Smithsonian Institution, and the Agricultural Department; to this list we are sorry to add the depot of the Baltimore and Potomac railroad. Original area, 227 acres, 8 perches.

Res. 3—The Park.—Bounded by 14th st. west on one side and the Potomac river on the other. This reservation is occupied by the Washington Monument and the Government nurseries. 29 acres, 3 roods, 9 perches.

Res. 4—The University Square.—On this reservation is situated the United States Naval Observatory. 21 acres, 18 perches.

Res. 5—The Arsenal Grounds.—This is at the foot of 4½ st. west, and is the most southern portion of Washington City. In 1857 this plat was extended by purchase. In the Penitentiary which stood here, but since removed, the conspirators adjudged guilty of Mr. Lincoln's murder were tried, and afterwards hung within its walls.

Res. 6—West Market-street Square.—This is at the foot of 20th and 21st sts. west, and is now covered with water.

Res. 7—Centre Market Square.—Occupied by the principal market in the city; 7th to 9th st. west, facing Pennsylvania avenue.

Res. 8—National Church Square.—Now occupied by Patent Office. Area, 4 acres, 22 perches. [See article, Patent Office, in this volume.]

Res. 9—Judiciary Square.—The site of the City Hall and surrounding grounds.

Res. 10.—North of Pennsylvania avenue, between 3d and 4½ sts. west. In 1822 Congress granted to the corporation the privilege of selling this reservation in lots to pay for the removal of the canal and to fill up the low grounds.

Res. 11.—Between B and C sts. north and 2d and 3d sts. west. Disposed of for the same purpose as Res. 10.

Res. 12.—North of Pennsylvania avenue, between 2d and 3d sts. west. Disposed of the same as Nos. 10 and 11. Area, 11 acres, 29 perches, of the reservations 10, 11, 12.

Res. 13—Hospital Square.—Between B and G sts. south, and 19th and the Anacostia east. Area, 77 acres, 26 perches. On it are the jail, the almshouse, and powder magazines.

Res. 14—The Navy-Yard.—Area, 12 acres, 3 roods, 15 perches.

Res. 15 and 16—Eastern Market-House Squares.—Near the Navy-yard, granted for market-house purposes. Area of the two reservations, 2 acres, 1 rood, 4 perches.

Res. 17—Town-House Square.—This is southeast of the Capitol, 3d st., and South Capitol st., where New Jersey, North Carolina, South Carolina, and Virginia avenues intersect, making an irregular plat with an area of 21 acres, 1 rood, 29 perches. The old

Duddington Manor-House, the residence of the Carroll family, fronts upon it. The Carroll spring, famous during the war times, is located here.

SQUARES, Etc.

There are a number of open squares in Washington City, besides those already alluded to as reservations; most of them are formed by the diverging lines of avenues intersecting other avenues and streets; they are of various sizes.

Lying West of the Capitol.

SCOTT SQUARE is formed by the intersection of Vermont avenue, 15th, I and K sts. n. w.; area, 1 acre 2 roods. The equestrian statue of Gen. McPherson is erected here. The cost of the pedestal on which it stands was $15,000.

FARRAGUT SQUARE is at the intersection of Connecticut avenue, 17th, I and K sts. n. w.; area, the same as Scott Square. In this square is to be placed, when completed, the colossal statue of Admiral Farragut, for which $20,000 was voted by Congress, April 16, 1872. Miss Ream received the order to make this statue.

Massachusetts and Rhode Island avenues intersect N st. and 16th st. about a quarter of a mile immediately north of the President's House, forming an open space of about an acre in extent. This square has no name, but is noted for the colossal equestrian bronze statue of GEN. SCOTT, which occupies its centre. The statue was designed by H. K. Brown, of New York, and cast by Robert Wood & Co., of Philadelphia. It weighs 12,000 lbs.; cost $20,000; weight of granite pedestal, over 320 tons. The cost of the pedestal was $53,000.

FRANKLIN SQUARE is bounded by 13th and 14th sts. west and by I and K sts. north. Government purchased this plat in 1829, because of its containing a fine spring, from which the President's House and Executive offices were supplied with water by pipes as early as 1832. The supply for the White House is still from this source.

Rawlins Square, on New York avenue, is southwest of the President's House, between 18th and 19th sts. n. w. Here is a bronze statue of Gen. John A. Rawlins, adjutant-general and chief-of-staff to Gen. Grant, who died Secretary of War. It cost $10,000. Designed by J. Bailey; cast by R. Wood & Co., Philadelphia.

Mount Vernon Place, at the intersection of K and 8th sts. n. w. with Massachusetts and New York avenues. A beautiful fountain occupies the centre. Until 1871 the Northern Market occupied this locality.

Fourteenth-street Circle, at the intersection of Massachusetts and Vermont avenues and 14th and M. sts. n. w., is beautifully laid out, and in the centre is a rustic fountain.

Thirteenth-street Circle is at the intersection of Vermont and Rhode Island avenues and P and 13th sts. n. w.

The Washington Circle is at the intersection of Pennsylvania and New Hampshire avenues and K and 23d sts. n. w., near Georgetown. Here is the equestrian bronze statue of Gen. Washington, by Clark Mills; cost $50,000. Cast out of captured guns donated by Congress.

P-street Circle is at the intersection of Connecticut, Massachusetts and New Hampshire avenues, at 19th and P sts. n. w. Near this is the house of the British Minister.

Lying East of the Capitol.

Stanton Place, still unimproved, is at the intersection of Maryland and Massachusetts avenues at 5th st. n. e., and embraces an area of 3 acres, 1 rood.

LINCOLN SQUARE is one mile directly east of the Capitol. Massachusetts, North Carolina, Tennessee, and Kentucky avenues here intersect between 11th and 13th sts. Originally it was intended to erect an *Historic Column* on this spot, which was also to serve as a *Mile* or *Itinerary Column*, from which all geographical distances in the United States were to be measured. Instead, however, is placed here the bronze group of EMANCIPATION, representing President Lincoln breaking the fetters of the slave, erected by the freedmen. Cost $17,000; inaugurated April 14, 1876; designed by Thomas Bell; cast at Munich by Von Müller, Jr.

THE AVENUES.

The avenues constitute a feature in the plan of WASHINGTON CITY calculated to confuse a stranger and to cause him at first to wonder much at their existence.

An early authority says:* "The positions for the different edifices, and for the several squares and areas, as laid down by the 'Geographer General,' Andrew Ellicott, [the contemporary and successor of Major L'Enfant,] were first determined on the most advantageous ground, commanding the most extensive prospects, and the better susceptible of such improvements as either use or ornament may require. *Lines of direct communication have been devised to connect the most distant objects with the principal by a direct communication with the main*, and preserving through the whole a reciprocity of sight and the most favorable ground for convenience and prospect."

L'Enfant, the originator of the idea, had, without doubt, the approaches to the palace of Versailles in his thoughts when he

* Jonathan Elliott in "Historical Sketches of the Ten Miles Square," pp. 98, 99.

conceived this feature in his plan of the Federal City, as in many respects they are almost a reproduction of the lines of those renowned *allées*.

The avenues are named after twenty-one of the States. To the old original Thirteen are added the names of Vermont, admitted 1791; Kentucky, 1792; Tennessee, 1796; Ohio, 1802; Louisiana, 1812; Indiana, 1816; Maine, 1820, and Missouri, 1821. Of course the avenues named after the later States were not contemplated in the original draft, and their introduction has not been, in the opinion of several recent writers, any improvement.

To attempt to describe the course of the various avenues would bewilder rather than instruct the reader. A reference to a map of Washington can alone enable the visitor to obtain any intelligent idea of the lines of their various directions. It might be well, however, to contradict a general error, often ignorantly asserted, that the avenues all radiate from the Capitol or the President's House. Although many of them diverge from these prominent buildings, quite a number of avenues do not approach either of them.

In 1871 Executive Avenue was devised. It encloses a portion of the grounds attached to the President's House, extending from 15½ to 16½ sts., and forms a semicircle south of the mansion; a broad single road starting from this centre, due south, enters the Drive opposite the Monument Grounds.

The following Tables, politely furnished by a gentleman connected with the office of the Commissioners of the District, will give very desirable information relative to the streets and the avenues:

State, War, and Navy Departments.

Treasury Department.

Table Showing the width of the Streets.

The streets running East and West are designated by letters of the alphabet, and by the word North or South, according as they are situated North or South of the Capitol, which is the dividing point; as A street north, A street south, which are the first streets north and south of the Capitol.

The streets running North and South are designated numerically, and by the word East or West, according to their position with respect to the Capitol; as First street east, and First street west.

	A	B	C	D	E	F	G	H	I	K	L	M	N	O	P	Q	R	S	T	U	V	W
North,	90	90	80	70	90	100	90	90	90	147.8	90	90	80	90	90	90	90	90	90	90	80	80
South,	90	90	80	90	90	70	100	80	90	80	90	90	90	85	85	85	85	85	85	80	80	40

	½	1	2	3	4	4½	5	6	7	8	9	10	11	12	13	13½	14	15	16	17	18	19	20	21	22	23	24	25	26	27	28
East,	80	110	90	90	85	—	100	85	90	100	90	80	90	112	90	—	100	90	80	100	80	80	100	80	80	80	80	—	—	—	—
West,	80	90	90	110	80	100	80	100	85	100	85	85	111.5	85	110	70	110	110	160	110	90	110	90	90	90	100	90	90	80	70	80

North and South Capitol streets, each 130 feet wide; East Capitol street, 160; Half streets, east and west, 80; Thirteen-and-a-Half street, 70; Water street, between South Capitol and W streets, 60 feet wide, elsewhere 80 feet; Boundary street, 80 feet wide. The streets on the East and West side of Lafayette Square are 90 feet wide: from F street north to the Mall, the width of Eighth street west is 85 feet 8 inches. The width of D street, northwest of Seventeenth street west, is 80 feet, elsewhere 70 feet.

The distance on an East and West line from the west side of Square No. 1 to the west side of Twenty-fourth street east, is 24,140.8 feet=4.572 miles. The distance on a North and South line, from the south side of W street south, along Eleventh street west to north side of Boundary street, is 19,954.8 feet=3.779 miles.

Table Showing the Course and Width of the Avenues.

Avenues.	*Width.*	*Course.*
Delaware	160 ft.	N. 15° 44′ E.
New Jersey	160 "	N. 15° 44′ W.
Maryland, east of Capitol	160 "	N. 62° 25′ E.
Maryland, west of Capitol	160 "	N. 70° 22′ 09″ E.
North Carolina	160 "	N. 62° 30′ E.
South Carolina	160 "	N. 71° 13′ 54″ E.
Georgia	160 "	N. 62° 30′ E.
Virginia, from Mall to Eastern Branch	160 "	S. 70° 18′ 05″ E.
Virginia, from Rock Creek to Potomac	120 "	S. 55° 20′ E.
Pennsylvania, from President's House to U. S. Capitol	160 "	S. 70° 33′ 30″ E.
Pennsylvania, west from President's House to Rock Creek	130 "	S. 66° E.
Pennsylvania, from Capitol to Eastern Branch	160 "	S. 62° 27′ E.
Kentucky	120 "	S. 33° E.
Tennessee	120 "	N. 32° 25′ E.
New York, east of President's House	130 "	N. 66° 09′ E.
New York, west of President's House	160 "	N. 70° 27′ E.
Vermont	130 "	N. 24° 31′ 30″ E.
Connecticut	130 "	N. 24° 31′ 30″ W.
Rhode Island	130 "	N. 66° E.
New Hampshire	120 "	N. 36° 09′ 14″ E.
Massachusetts, west of New Jersey avenue	160 "	S. 66° 03′ E.
Massachusetts, east of New Jersey avenue	160 "	S. 62° 26′ 08″ E.
Ohio	160 "	S. 70° 18′ E.
Louisiana	160 "	S. 70° 21′ 36″ W.
Indiana	160 "	S. 70° 23′ 30″ E.
Missouri	85 "	S. 70° 33′ 30″ E.
Maine	85 "	N. 70° 22′ 09″ E.

As a general rule, until within a few years the Public Buildings were accessible daily to visitors from 9 A. M. to 3 P. M. The increase of service demanded in the various Departments has caused some change in this arrangement, and the following regulations, subject perhaps to slight temporary changes dependent upon an increase of work in a particular Bureau or Department, are now observed. A knowledge of them will enable a stranger who is pressed for time to plan his round of visits with greater satisfaction to himself:

THE CAPITOL is open during daytime every day excepting Sunday, and at night time when Congress has a night session. The CONGRESSIONAL LIBRARY from 9 A. M. to 4 P. M., and the BOTANICAL GARDENS every week day.

THE PRESIDENT'S HOUSE.—The East-Room is open every week day from 10 A. M. to 3 P. M.

We will mention the other more important places in alphabetical order:

AGRICULTURAL BUILDING is open from 9 A. M. to 3 P. M.; also, the ARMY MEDICAL MUSEUM. ARLINGTON CEMETERY is open every day, Sunday included.

CORCORAN ART-GALLERY, 17th st. and Pennsylvania avenue n. w., is open daily from 10 A. M. to 4 P. M. Mondays, Wednesdays, and Fridays are *pay* days. The three other days, admission is *free.*

INSANE ASYLUM is open on Wednesdays from 2 to 6 P. M.

INTERIOR DEPARTMENT, including the Model-Room, Patent Office, is open daily from 9 A. M. to 4 P. M. The DEPARTMENT OF JUSTICE is also open until 4 P. M.

NAVY DEPARTMENT is open daily from 9 A. M. to 4 P. M. The NAVY YARD is open daily from 9 A. M. to sunset.

SMITHSONIAN INSTITUTION, open daily from 9 A. M. to 4 P. M.

SOLDIERS' HOME is open daily from 9 to dark. Carriages admitted to the grounds excepting on Sundays.

STATE DEPARTMENT, open daily, except on Thursdays, (appropriated to foreign diplomats,) from 10 A. M. to 2 P. M.

TREASURY DEPARTMENT is open from 9 A. M. to 2 P. M.

WAR DEPARTMENT is open from 9 A. M. to 3 P. M.

PRESIDENT'S HOUSE.

The President's House is about a mile and a half from the Capitol, in a direction west by north. It stands between 15th and 17th sts. n. w., on a high plateau, where Pennsylvania and New York avenues intersect, and fronting it is Lafayette Square. It is built of a yellowish freestone painted white, and is popularly known as **The White House.**

It is two stories high, 170 feet long, and 86 feet wide, with a portico on the north, supported by eight pillars, under which carriages can drive. The south front has a semicircular colonnade of six columns in the centre. A conservatory adjoins the house on the west.

The building is said to have been modelled after the palace of the Duke of Leinster, in Dublin. The architect was James Hoban, an Irishman, who came to Washington from Charleston, South Carolina.

First Floor.

The north door opens into a vestibule 40 by 50 feet, divided by a sash screen; within the screen are portraits of Adams, Van Buren, Tyler, Polk, Fillmore, and Pierce.

The East-Room, occupying the eastern side of the house, is 80 by 40 feet, and 22 feet high. The ceiling is divided into three panels, beautifully decorated. The chandeliers, mirrors, and furniture are of the most elegant description. It is, as a rule, accessible to the public. Here is Stewart's Washington and Jefferson, with Cogswell's Lincoln.

Adjoining the East-Room, west, is the Green-Room, facing the south, so called from the dominant color of its furniture, all of which is exceedingly beautiful; 30 by 20 feet.

Then succeeds the Blue-Room. This is of oval shape, with windows looking southward; and, as its name indicates, is furnished in *blue* and gold; 40 by 30 feet. This is the room in which, at *levees*, the President receives his guests.

The room next, still facing south, which brings you gradually towards the western side of the house, is the RED-ROOM. This room is used more commonly by the presidential family, and has somewhat of a home look about it; 30 by 20 feet.

Then, in the southwest portion of the house, is the STATE DINING-ROOM, 40 by 30 feet. This is fitted up in admirable style, and is only used on state occasions. The private dining-room is north of the state dining-room.

Second Floor.

The east part is occupied by the Executive offices, ante-rooms, and the PRESIDENT'S OFFICE. In this last the Cabinet meets. It is spacious, and commands a beautiful view looking south. Adjoining it is the library. The rooms occupied by the family are in the south and western portions of the house, and are mainly used as bed-chambers.

Basement Floor.

This contains the kitchens, servants' quarters, store-rooms, and depositories for coal, etc.

History.

The corner-stone of the President's House was laid October 13, 1792; architect, James Hoban. It was first occupied in 1800, by President John Adams, but was then in an unfinished condition. The building cost, up to 1814, $333,207. August 24, of that year, the President's House was burned by the British. It was authorized to be rebuilt in 1815. Mr. Hoban was again charged with its erection, according to the original plan, and its re-erection cost $301,496.25. It was first again occupied by President Monroe.

The STABLES and CONSERVATORY attached to the President's House cost $72,079.82.

Lafayette Square.

This beautiful square is in front (north) of the White House, and includes seven acres. Two bronze vases, the copy of an antique, seven feet high, and weighing each 1,300 lbs., ornament the grounds.

The **Equestrian Statue of Gen. Andrew Jackson**, designed and cast by Clark Mills, is also here. The Jackson Monument Association subscribed $12,000, and Congress granted captured guns for the casting of this statue; afterwards other appropriations were made, including a sum of $20,000, the whole netting about $50,000. Its weight is 15 tons.

STATE DEPARTMENT.

This magnificent structure, now being erected, was designed by A. B. Mullett, late Supervising Architect of the Treasury. It is intended to accommodate the State, War, and Navy Departments. The south end of the building only is completed, and is, since 1875, occupied by the State Department. It is immediately west of the President's House.

It is 342 feet from east to west, including projections, etc., and will be 567 feet from north to south. The style is the Italian renaissance; the material of which it is built is granite, brought from Maine and Virginia; the roof is mansard. The building was begun in 1871. The expenditures to date, 1876, including furniture, are $4,230,062.96.

The interior is superbly finished and furnished, and there are documents, etc., deposited here of great interest.

On the second floor are the RECEPTION-ROOM, the ROOM OF THE

Secretary of State, and the rooms of the Assistant Secretaries and Chief Clerk.

The Library, embracing the most complete and valuable collection of works on diplomacy in America, is in the third story, over the south entrance.

There are extensive files in the Department of American newspapers from 1781.

TREASURY DEPARTMENT.

On the east side of the President's House stands the United States Treasury.

It has four fronts, each facing a point of the compass. These, including porticos and steps, measure 582 feet by 300 feet. The front first built was the east front; it is of Virginia freestone, and presents an extended colonnade. Mr. Robert Mills was the architect of this portion of the building. The rest is of granite from Dix Island, Maine.

The west, north, and south fronts correspond with each other, having each a central projecting portico. The architects, Walter, Young, Rogers, and Mullet, were all engaged on this splendid edifice. The cost, as stated in a recent report, is $6,837,722.28; the usual amount stated is $6,000,000.

The Treasury contains 195 rooms, to which is to be added those in the sub-basement, used for store-rooms, shops, and those attached to the heating apparatus. Besides, are the rooms in the *attic story*, used by the Bureau of Engraving and Printing, in which about 500 persons are employed. The machinery is driven by a 100 horse-power engine.

The Cash-Room is the most beautiful of any in the Treasury, and well worth a visit. The display of foreign marbles in this room is very fine, but to an American it would be more satisfactory had they been of native origin.

THE VAULTS are of steel and chilled iron: they are situated in the northeast part of the Treasury. They are about 15 by 20 feet in size. Two of them are in the basement.

PHOTOGRAPH OFFICE. This is a small cottage-like looking building opposite the south front of the Treasury. Here are photographed *fac similes* of accounts, plans and elevations of public buildings, etc., etc.

Coast Survey.

This building is private property, although built for the special service of this office. It is south of the Capitol, on New Jersey avenue, between B and C sts., and is an imposing brick structure.

The object of this office is "the survey of the coasts of the United States on tide-water." It originated in 1807, but its actual organization was completed in 1833.

The standards of weights and measures are kept here, under the care of the Superintendent. The Coast Survey is attached to the Treasury Department. Its duties, however, are mainly discharged "by officers of the army and navy, with the assistance of scientific civilians."

History.

In 1814 the U. S. Treasury shared the general fate of the public buildings, and was burned on the invasion of the city. The structure again erected for its use occupied the site of the southern portion of the present edifice; it was, however, consumed by fire March 31, 1833. It is said President Jackson indicated with his cane the site of the existing structure. In 1836 it was commenced, and made ready to be occupied in 1841. In 1855 the Extension was begun. The north front was the last one completed. It is now proposed to remove the east front and substitute another, in conformity with the rest of the edifice.

Executive Mansion, North Front.

Executive Mansion, South Front.

Soldiers' Home.

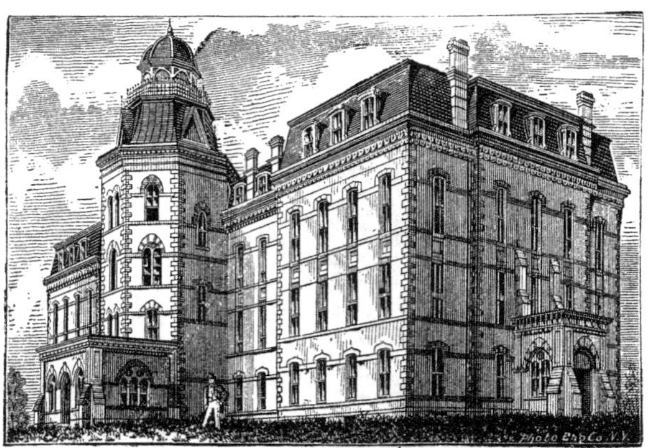

Howard University.

WAR DEPARTMENT.

The War Department, a very plain-looking building facing north, is on the west side of the President's House, at the corner of 17th st. n.w. The intention is to remove the present structure, and extend the magnificent new building close by, now in course of erection, so that within it accommodation will be afforded, not only to the State Department, but to the War and Navy Departments.

The Secretary's Office is on the second story, in the east side of the building. A collection of portraits of the Secretaries of War is here, as well as a number of interesting relics, manuscripts, etc.

The headquarters of the General of the Army are, since the return from St. Louis to Washington, again located on the first floor east of the main hall, in the same suite of rooms previously so occupied, in the north front of the building.

For many years the room accommodation of the Department has not been sufficient for its need, and outside quarters have been appropriated.

The **Signal Office** is on the north side of G street, west of the War Department. Entrance, No. 1719.

The Flag-room is at No. 616 17th st., opposite the Department.

The Quartermaster-General's Office is at the corner of 15th st. and Pennsylvania avenue, diagonally opposite the front of the Treasury. That of the Surgeon-General of the Army is on Pennsylvania avenue, opposite the north front of the Treasury.

The Army Medical Museum

is on 10th st. n. w., midway between E and F sts. n. w. To the medical student it is interesting beyond expression. The building was once **Ford's Theatre**, in which President Lincoln was assassinated. Its purchase cost $88,000.

Winder's Building,

corner of 17th and F sts. n. w., was originally built for a hotel, but was purchased and fitted up for the use of Government at an expense of $246,054.78. It is variously occupied.

The CHIEF-ENGINEER OF THE ARMY occupies the first floor. The BATTLE-RECORD ROOM is No. 2, and No. 13 is a FILE-ROOM for papers of the ADJUTANT-GENERAL'S OFFICE.

The JUDGE-ADVOCATE GENERAL OF THE ARMY occupies the front portion of the second story.

The ORDNANCE OFFICE also is on the second floor, connected with which is an exceedingly interesting MUSEUM.

The rooms above are used by the SECOND AUDITOR OF THE TREASURY.

The Arsenal

is at the foot of 4½ st. s. w., and is accessible by horse rail-cars. The grounds are beautifully laid out, and many objects of interest are here open for inspection. As early as 1803 it was a military station, and in 1814 it was one of the places destroyed by the British. In 1815, under Col. George Bomford, it was rebuilt. The Chief of Ordnance resides here. (See **Reservation** No. 5.)

SOLDIERS' HOME.

This institution is, in object, somewhat similar to that of the *Hotel des Invalides* at Paris. To Gen. Winfield Scott is the military service indebted, in great part, for the suggestion and endowment of the Soldiers' Home.

March 3, 1851, not long after the termination of the Mexican war, Congress donated $118,719, the unused balance in the Treasury of the sum levied by Gen. Scott on the City of Mexico, to aid in the establishment of the Home. To this sum is added forfeitures, stoppages, and fines, and a tax of 12 cts. a month (formerly 25 cts.) on each private soldier.

The main building is of marble, 200 ft. front. There are also several beautiful marble cottages, the residences of the officers, and the former Riggs' homestead, clustered near it.

In summer time Presidents Pierce, Buchanan, and Lincoln resided here. A new hospital also has recently been erected within the grounds.

There is here, on the brow of the hill, a bronze statue of *Gen. Scott*, 10 ft. high, facing the city, by Launt Thompson, erected by the Home in 1874; cost $18,000.

The grounds embrace 500 acres, and are most beautifully laid out. The drive within the enclosure extends 7 miles.

Disabled private soldiers of the regular army are entitled to the benefits of the Home; during their stay their pensions are stopped.

The Home is three miles north of the Capitol. The tower of the main building affords the most beautiful of views, the Capitol being a main feature in the landscape. On a clear day the top of Sugar-Loaf mountain can be discerned in the far distance.

Horse-cars connect with, and convey passengers from, the terminus of the Seventh-street route to within a short distance of the Home.

National Military Cemetery.

This burial-place adjoins the Soldiers' Home; established in 1861. It is a sad memorial of the war; 5,153 Union and 271 Confederate dead are interred here. The names of 279 of them are unknown.

NAVY DEPARTMENT.

Immediately south of the War Department is a building of the same general plain description, which is the UNITED STATES NAVY DEPARTMENT. The original building faced south, but a needed wing gives it now the appearance of its main front facing west.

The SECRETARY'S OFFICE is on the second floor, at the south end of the corridor.

The ADMIRAL'S OFFICE is at his residence, 1710 H street n. w.

The HYDROGRAPHIC OFFICE (established in 1866, is a branch of the Bureau of Navigation) occupies the "Octagon," a house built by the Tayloe family, and considered for many years one of the most elegant of the private residences in Washington city. It is at the n. e. corner of 18th street and New York avenue n. w.

The NAUTICAL ALMANAC OFFICE, also a branch of the Bureau of Navigation, is on Twenty-second street n. w., No. 807.

The service of the Naval Department is divided into eight Bureaus, viz: Ordnance, Equipment and Recruiting, Yards and Docks, Navigation, Medicine and Surgery, Provisions and Clothing, Steam Engineering, and Construction and Repair.

National Observatory.

On a hill 96 feet high, southwest from the President's House, on the Potomac river, is situated the National Observatory, near the s. w. terminus of New York avenue.

This hill, long ago, was known as *Peter's Hill*, having belonged to Mr. Robert Peter, one of the original proprietors. It was also called *Camp Hill*, because the forces of Gen. Braddock encamped here previous to starting on the ill-fated expedition of 1755; and in 1814 the troops mustered to defend Washington were stationed here. It was embraced within the proposed town of Hamburg or Funkstown, laid out and lots therein sold years before the Federal city was devised, and the titles to which became sources of annoyance to the early commissioners.

Gen. Washington was desirous of having a national university established here. [See **Reservation** No. 4.]

The Observatory is under the direction of the Navy Department, and belongs to the Bureau of Navigation. It was established in 1842. The central building was completed in 1844. Its present rank is among the foremost in the world. There is here, mounted in 1873, the most powerful telescope ever made, the "Great Equatorial;" cost $47,000. It weighs, including its base, six tons. The cost of the iron dome erected to cover it was $14,000.

The Naval Hospital

is between 9th and 10th sts., on Pennsylvania avenue east; it is attached to the Bureau of Medicine and Surgery of the Navy Department, and is for the benefit of the officers and men of the Navy and the Marine Corps. Cost $116,935.33.

Navy-Yard.

At the southern terminus of 8th st. east is the entrance to the Washington Navy-Yard. It lies along the banks of the Anacostia.

Dec. 30, 1799, Hon. Benj. Stoddard, Secretary of the Navy, ordered the grounds to be laid out. The yard was formally established by act of March, 1804. The grounds occupy about 27 acres.

It contains a large number of trophies connected with our naval encounters, and is well worth a visit.

The MUSEUM, open from 9 A. M. to 4 P. M., is full of objects of interest. There is here a Spanish gun which Cortez used in his conquest of Mexico, obtained during our Mexican war, and a small mortar captured from Lord Cornwallis, etc., etc.

The *Wasp*, the *Argus*, the *Viper*, the *Shark* and *Grampus*, the sloop *St. Louis*, 24 guns, and frigates *Columbia*, *Essex*, *Po-*

tomac, and *Brandywine*, of 44 guns each, and the *Columbus*, of 74 guns, were built here. Recently the yard has been more prominent for its manufacture of naval supplies than for naval construction. Its workshops are extensive.

The Marine Barracks

are of brick, and occupy the whole of square 927, a short distance north of the entrance to the Navy-Yard, on 8th st., between G and I sts. s.e.

The barracks were burnt in 1814 by the British, but were immediately rebuilt. The architect was Mr. Latrobe. Cost $335,-636.81.

The Marine Corps, created in 1798, is an adjunct to the Navy. The headquarters are in Washington. The force consists of a Commandant holding the rank of brigadier-general, 1 colonel, 2 lieutenant-colonels, 4 majors, 20 captains, with a larger number of lieutenants, and about 2,500 men.

POST-OFFICE DEPARTMENT.

This building occupies the whole square between 7th and 8th and E and F sts. n. w., and is opposite the Patent Office. It is of white marble, from New York and Maryland quarries, and is of a modified Corinthian order of architecture. It is said to be the best representation of the Italian palatial in America, and recalls remembrance of a Florentine palace. It measures 300 feet north and south, and 204 feet east and west. It cost, up to 1876, $1,855,889.59.

In the centre of the front facing 8th st., over the carriage gateway, is an interesting specimen of carving, representing "the railroad and the telegraph."

The City Post-Office is in the centre of the north front.

The Postmaster-General's Office is in the story above the basement, on the south side

THE DEAD-LETTER OFFICE is on the north side. To enter this requires a pass, which is easily obtained from the Chief Clerk.

History.

The site of the south side of the Post-Office Department was, early in the history of Washington city, occupied by a brick building, projected by Samuel Blodgett, an unsuccessful speculator, for a hotel. It was to be 120 ft. long, 50 ft. wide, and three stories high. James Hoban was architect. The corner-stone was laid in 1793, and the plan approved by the commissioners.

It "was put up," as Watterson states, "out of the proceeds of a lottery authorized to be drawn, but not completed. The owners of the prize-ticket were orphan children, who, not having the means of completing the building, suffered it to remain in an unfinished and dilapidated state." It was here the first theatrical entertainments were given in the national Capital.

In 1810 it was bought by Government, and plainly finished.

Congress, in 1814–'15, after the burning of the Capitol, held one session here; and in the second story the Patent Office was for years accommodated. The lower story was occupied by the General and City Post-Offices until Dec. 15, 1836, when the building was destroyed by fire. Private buildings were then rented for the immediate need.

In 1839 the south portion of the present building was commenced by Robert Mills. Government bought the north half of the square to F st. in 1842. In 1855 the new Extension was begun. The designs were made by Thomas U. Walter, architect of the Capitol, and executed by Capt., now Gen. M. C. Meigs, and Edward Clark, architect.

DEPARTMENT OF THE INTERIOR.

Patent Office.

The Patent Office building, in which much of the work connected with the Department of the Interior is performed, covers two squares—from 7th to 9th sts. and from F to G sts n. w. It measures 410 feet from east to west, and 275 feet from north to south. It is Doric in architecture, and in the original plan of the city the ground on which it stands was reserved for the building of a grand National Church.

The present structure was commenced in 1837. The south front—built of freestone, painted white—was the earliest built; designed by Wm. F. Elliot, and executed by Robert Mills. The east wing was authorized in 1849, was commenced by Mr. Mills, who was succeeded, in 1851, by Edward Clark, then assistant to the architect of the Capitol, by whom the building was completed in 1864. The new portions are of Maryland marble or the street extensions and granite on the interior quadrangle. The building contains about 191 rooms, and cost $2,700,000.

Four halls on the second floor compass the whole extent of the vast building, and have on exhibition the model of every patent issued since 1836.

There are also here many articles which belonged to Gen. Washington possessing historical interest, and here is to be seen the original Declaration of Independence.

In December, 1836, a fire consumed the building then occupied by the Patent Office, situated where the General Post Office now stands. The models accumulated during 46 years were all destroyed. The patents to that date numbered 10,301. From July 4, 1836, to July 4, 1876, there were issued 179,638 patents.

In this building is the office of the Secretary of the Interior, who has charge of affairs "connected with patents, public lands,

Agricultural Department.

Smithsonian.

Washington's Tomb at Mount Vernon.

Arlington House.

pensions, Indians, census, education, and beneficiary asylums in the District; and he has also supervisory control over the architect of the Capitol." The immense structure is not large enough to accommodate all the offices connected with the Department, and several rented buildings have necessarily been brought into its service.

The **Bureau of Education** is located at the corner of G and 8th sts. n. w., opposite the north front of the Patent Office. The Department of Education was created March 2, 1867. Its design is to collect statistics and facts showing the condition and progress of education in the States and Territories. The following year it was reduced to a *bureau*, called the "Office of Education."

Survey of the Territories.—Office on 7th st., between E and F sts. n. w. Here information can be obtained relative to the surveys in the far West, and photographs seen illustrative of the work of the various scientific exploring expeditions of the United States.

Pension Bureau, cor. Pennsylvania ave. and 12th st. n. w.

Government Hospital for the Insane.

On the high ground on the south side of the Anacostia is this institution. In the distance it looks like a large feudal castle. There is attached to it an estate of 419 acres, a portion of which is cultivated by the patients. Miss Dix, the well-known philanthropist, took an active part in urging the establishment of this great Government benevolence. Nearly one thousand persons, [illegible]ttendants and patients, are accommodated within its walls. It [illegible]so known as the St. Elizabeth Hospital. The Institution [illegible]ned in 1855. It is 750 feet long. Cost of building, etc., [illegible]5; support, etc., of insane paupers, as reported to [illegible].846.35.

An iron bridge across the Anacostia, near the Navy Yard, affords access to the Insane Hospital. Its reported cost is $99,487.00.

Columbia Institution for the Deaf and Dumb

is situated on "Kendall Green," lying in a northeasterly direction from the Capitol; entrance, north end of 7th st. east, also the east terminus of M st. north. Amos Kendall, Postmaster-General in Gen. Jackson's Cabinet, donated, late in life, some acres and a small building, first occupied by the institution, which was incorporated in 1857, and since mainly supported by Congress. In 1864 a collegiate department was created. It has since rapidly increased in efficiency. In 1870, the Board purchased an additional 82 acres of Kendall Green property, for $85,000, payable in four years. The property is valued at $350,000.

Columbia Hospital for Women, and Lying-in Asylum, corner of L and 25th sts. n. w. Supported mainly by Government. Appropriations to present time, (1876,) $173,495.46. A *dispensary* is open here every day.

DEPARTMENT OF JUSTICE.

Opposite the United States Treasury is a splendid building, originally erected for the Freedman's Bank. Its upper stories are occupied by this Department; entrance at west end.

The principal object of interest here is the gallery of portraits of the Attorneys-General of the United States.

This Department was created June, 1870. The head is the United States Attorney-General; all Government prosecutions are conducted by it. Subordinate to it are the officers of the District and Circuit Courts of the United States; the Reform School; Metropolitan Police and jail of the District of Columbia, and the various law officers of the national Departments.

The Court-House, (formerly the City Hall,)

is situated opposite the northern terminus of 4½ street, on Judiciary Square, which comprises about 20 acres. The courts of the District are held, excepting that of the Police Court, in the Court-House.

The structure is of freestone, painted white. It was designed by George Hadfield, an Englishman, one of the architects of the Capitol. Only about one-half of the building, as designed by him, has been erected. It was commenced in 1820; whole frontage, 250 feet.

In front of the building, on a marble column, is a statue of PRESIDENT LINCOLN, by Lot Flannery, of Washington city, erected by contributions of citizens. (See **Reservation** No. 9.)

The POLICE COURT is located on C st., between 4½ and 6th sts. n. w.

The Reform School

is situated on LINCOLN'S HILL, (a fort of that name occupying the site during the war of the rebellion,) on the Washington and Baltimore turnpike, about two miles from the east boundary of the city. It is solely for boys, and is surrounded by a farm of 150 acres.

DEPARTMENT OF AGRICULTURE.

Between the Smithsonian Institution and the Washington Monument grounds is situated the Agricultural Department, between 12th and 14th sts. s. w. It is of brick, with brownstone trimmings; 170 feet long, 61 feet deep; designed by Adolph Cluss, and has a Mansard roof; finished in 1868. It bears a resemblance to what the Palace of Versailles was when only a hunting chateau, before Louis XIV expended upon it the revenues of a kingdom.

There are extensive structures built for experimental gardening, known as *Plant-Houses*, designed by Mr. Saunders, "Superintendent of Gardens," etc. The main building is 320 feet long and 30 feet wide, with a projecting centre wing 150 feet long.

Besides the gardens, etc., there is here an *Agricultural Museum* of great interest. The buildings and grounds cost, to 1875, $541,243.25.

The Department was established May 15, 1862. Before occupying the present building, it had rooms in the basement of the Patent Office, and was, as a Bureau, under the supervision of the Secretary of the Interior.

THE GOVERNMENT PRINTING OFFICE.

is at the corner of North Capitol and H sts.; length, 300 feet on H st. and 175 feet on North Capitol st.; it is 4 stories high, and cost (the building) $84,915.74. It is said to be at present the largest printing establishment in the world.

In 1852, a change was made in the then contract system of public printing and binding, and the office created of Superintendent of Public Printing.

In 1860, Congress bought of Cornelius Wendell for $135,000 his printing office, which became the nucleus of the present mammoth establishment. In 1867, the office of "Superintendent," etc., was abolished, and the Senate authorized to elect a practical printer to take charge of the Government work.

Washington Asylum, etc.

This institution is an asylum for the poor, and a workhouse for those convicted of minor crimes, except theft, in the police courts. It is situated on Hospital Square, or Reservation 13, devoted to that and kindred purposes, being the extreme eastern portion of the city. The first building was put up in 1815; there are now accommodations for 180 persons.

North of it is the new District Jail, four stories high, 310 by 193 feet, designed by A. B. Mullett. Cost $343,556.77. Begun in 1872; made ready for occupation in 1875. The Army and Navy Magazines are in near neighborhood, and south of them is the beautiful

Congressional Cemetery.

This Cemetery is attached to Christ Church, Episcopal, (Washington parish,) Navy-Yard. (See Churches.)

The Cemetery now embraces 30 acres. It was laid out in 1807, with about 10 acres. It is called Congressional because there are sites allotted here for the interment of members of Congress who die in office, and even if not buried here, a monument is erected to the memory of such. There are rows of tombs, many of which are empty. It is not only beautiful as a cemetery, but is interesting on account of the many distinguished dead who lie here. Congress has made donations to this Cemetery of $28,670.59.

Smithsonian Institution.

The Smithsonian Institution is built of red-freestone, and has numerous towers, reminding one of the palace of the old Scotch kings, Holyrood. The extreme length of the building, from east to west, is 447 feet; the breadth of the centre, including carriage-porch, is 160 feet. It was designed by James Renwick, Jr., of New York. The style is Norman, in use about the end of the 12th century; corner-stone laid 1847; completed 1856; cost $450,000.

The grounds, extending from 7th to 12th streets, were laid out by Andrew Jackson Downing, a landscape gardener of great reputation, who died while prosecuting this work. There is a beautiful vase to his memory erected here.

This Institution is the bequest of an English gentleman,

James Smithson, an illegitimate son of a Duke of Northumberland. Mr. Smithson was born in London, and graduated, taking an honorary degree, at Oxford in 1786. He was a skilful chemist, mineralogist, and geologist, and was the author of valuable treatises on these various subjects. The bequest was "*to found at Washington, under the name of the Smithsonian Institution, an establishment for the increase and diffusion of knowledge among men.*" The original bequest was $515,169. In 1836 Congress accepted it, and it was obtained through Hon. Richard Rush, of Pennsylvania, designated a commissioner for the purpose. The accumulated interest, etc., was sufficient to pay for the erection of the building.

The *National Museum* deposited here includes the collections of all the exploring expeditions of the United States, besides all other sorts of curiosities, and would require weeks to examine carefully.

The Institution publishes and distributes original works on *General* and *Special Science*, and is engaged in extensive *Meteorological Investigations.* The Library, once centered here, has been removed to the Capitol into a hall of the Library of Congress.

Washington Monument.

This, in 1876, is an incomplete white marble obelisk, situated on a bluff on the Potomac river, near the northwest terminus of Virginia avenue. It is the spot where Gen. Washington indicated his choice for the erection of the statue which the Continental Congress had voted in honor of his services. (See **Reservation** No. 3.)

In 1835 the Washington Monument Association was formed. Chief-Justice Marshall was its first president. Its object was to erect a monument to the memory of our great first President. The accepted design was the idea of Robert Mills: a shaft rising from a rotunda to the height of 600 feet—designed to be the highest structure ever reared by man, excepting the Tower of Babel.

The corner-stone was laid July 4, 1848. Ex-President John Quincy Adams was to have delivered the address, but his death occurring a few months previous, Robert C. Winthrop, of Massachusetts, Speaker of the House of Representatives, was selected to perform that duty. The amount collected was $230,000.

The funds were exhausted and work suspended before the late civil war culminated; and, although efforts have been again and again made to resume its construction, they have, thus far, been unsuccessful.

It is now proposed that the shaft shall reach only 485 feet, 174 of which are already completed.

In the *lapidarium*, i. e., a collection of ornamental blocks of marble, etc., presented by nations, States, societies of different kinds, etc., are 83 memorial stones, with various inscriptions and designs chiselled upon them, intended to be placed in the interior of the monument, arranged for inspection within a building on the premises. Besides, 40 memorial stones are already inserted within the structure. Visitors are admitted, and an examination of them will repay the traveller.

It is with pleasure we record that Congress, by joint resolution, has, in 1876, resolved to provide funds to complete the monument.

Corcoran Gallery of Art.

At the corner of 17th street and Pennsylvania avenue, opposite the War Department, is the Corcoran Gallery of Art. It is in the renaissance style, 104 feet by 124½ feet, of brick, with trimmings of Belleville freestone. The building is the gift of Mr. W. W. Corcoran, a retired wealthy banker and philanthropist of Washington, to the United States. With it was also given his own private art collection, and an endowment fund of $900,000, the interest on which is to be expended to increase the value of the collection. Facilities for copying the works of the Gallery are cordially extended to artists and students. An admirable Catalogue has been published of this art collection, which of itself is a valuable compendium of art information, compiled by the curator, Mr. Wm. Macleod.

It is open daily, but on Mondays, Wednesdays, and Fridays there is a charge of 25 cents entrance; on Tuesdays, Thursdays, and Saturdays the admission is free. The gallery of sculpture and bronzes is exceedingly fine, and very valuable.

Masonic Temple

is at the corner of 9th and F sts. n. w., opposite the Patent Office. Corner-stone laid 1868. Cost $200,000. Built of granite and Connecticut and Nova Scotia freestone.

The Order was early planted in the Federal City. Prior to 1816 two Lodges assembled in a building near the river.

Odd-Fellows' Hall

is on 7th st., between D and E sts. n. w. It was dedicated in 1846; remodelled in 1873. The first Lodge of the Order was established in the District in 1827; the Grand Lodge followed in 1828.

Providence Hospital.

This hospital was founded in 1862 by the Sisters of Charity. Government has appropriated, as stated in a recent report, 1876, principally towards the erection of this building, through the exertions of Thaddeus Stevens, $60,000; and there is still continued an annual appropriation for 75 non-resident pauper patients. Its accommodations for pay patients are excellent; and

Insane Asylum.

Cabin-John Bridge.

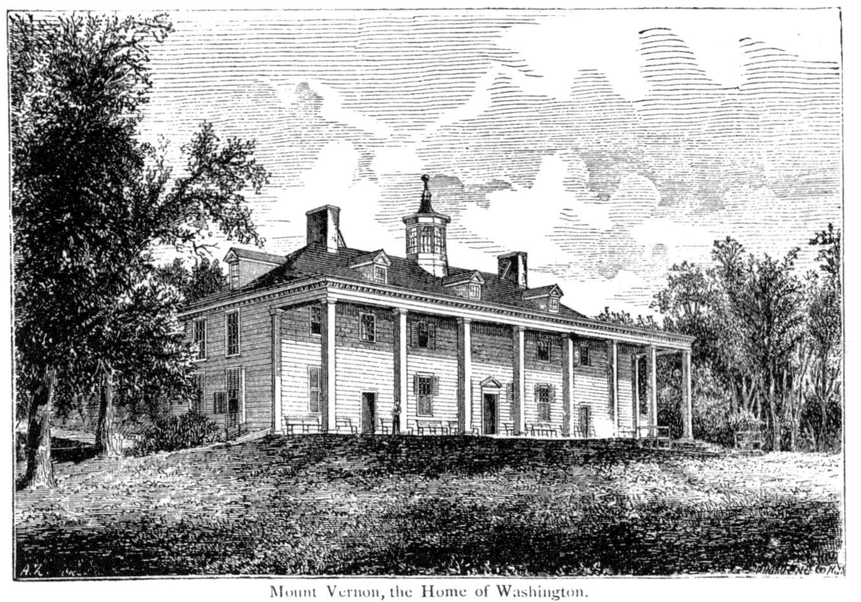

Mount Vernon, the Home of Washington.

it has attached to it a library, reading-room, and chapel. It is situated at the corner of D and 2d sts. s. e.

Armory.

In 1855, $30,000 was appropriated for the erection of a building for the storing and care of the ordnance, etc., of the United States, required for the use of volunteers and militia of the District. The building erected for this purpose stands on the public reservation (the Mall) near 6th st.

Early in the breaking out of the war it was used as a hospital, and gave name to one of the most extensive and useful of the army hospitals, clustered in several wooden buildings, near its site.

Gonzaga College

was founded a seminary in 1848; incorporated a university in 1858; is conducted by fathers of the Society of Jesus. It is on I st., between North Capitol and First st. n. w.

Columbian University

is situated on a hill a short distance from the northern terminus of the 14th st. horse-railroad route. The grounds embrace 40 acres; the estimated value of estate $400,000. It was founded by the Baptists; incorporated in 1821; commenced in 1822. During the recent war it was used for hospital purposes.

In 1873 it became a University. The President of the United States and the Chief-Justice of the Supreme Court are honorary members of the Board of Trustees.

The *National Medical College*, connected with the University, is on H st., between 13th and 14th sts. n. w.; founded in 1824. The building, in 1864, was presented by Mr. W. W. Corcoran.

The *Law Department*, established 1826, is on 5th st., between D and E sts. n. w., opposite Judiciary square.

Howard University

occupies a commanding situation on a hill near the northern terminus of the 7th st. horse-railroad route. It was incorporated in 1867, and named in compliment after Gen. Howard, then director of the Freedmen's Bureau. The admission, etc., of pupils is without regard to sex or color. The value of property is about $600,000.

Freedmen's Asylum.

This is in the near neighborhood of Howard University; and in the list of expenditures of Government to 1875 is stated as having cost for its support $207,716.90.

Wayland Seminary.

In 1865 this institution was founded for the purpose of educating *colored preachers and teachers.* It is situated near Columbian University. The seminary is three stories high, of brick, with mansard roof and tower; cost $35,000. It is one of seven schools supported in the South by the American Baptist Home Mission Society.

BENEVOLENT INSTITUTIONS.

National Soldiers and Sailors Orphans' Home, G st., between 17th and 18th sts. n. w.; incorporated in 1866; amount appropriated by Government $77,381.25; under the charge of a board of lady managers. No applicants received under six years old, nor kept after 16 years.

Louise Home, on Massachusetts avenue, between 15th and 16th sts. n. w.; built in 1871. It provides an elegant home for reduced gentlewomen, and is the gift of the wealthy Washingtonian, Mr. W. W. Corcoran, who has called it by the name of his wife and daughter, ladies now dead. It cost $200,000, and has an endowment of $250,000. It accommodates 55 persons. The inmates are invited by the lady directresses. Open to visitors every week day, after 12 noon.

Washington City Orphan Asylum, corner of 14th and S sts. n. w.; founded in 1815. Dolly Madison was first directress, and Mrs. Van Ness (Marcia Burns) second. Incorporated in 1828. It is under the control of benevolent Protestant ladies of the city.

Children's Hospital, on E st., between 8th and 9th sts. n. w.; incorporated in 1871. Its object is to provide free surgical and medical treatment for the poor children of the District. It is under the patronage of the benevolent. A *free dispensary* is connected with it. Sundays, Tuesdays, and Fridays, from 3 to 5 P. M., are visiting days.

St. John's Hospital, for children; under the direction of the St. John Sisterhood of the Episcopal Church. The new house is on H. st., between 19th and 20th sts. n. w. Received an appropriation from Government of $25,000.

St. Ann's Infant Asylum; founded 1863; for children less than five years; under the management of the Sisters of Charity. A *lying-in hospital* is attached. Corner of K and 24th sts. n. w. Visiting day, Thursday, from 2 to 5 P. M.

St Joseph's Male Orphan Asylum; founded 1855; under the care of the Sisters of the Holy Cross; is on H st., between 9th and 10th sts. n. w.

St. Vincent's Female Orphan Asylum; founded 1831; under the care of the Sisters of Charity; is on the s. w. corner of G and 10th sts. n. w. A branch, known as **St. Rose's Orphan Home,** is on G st., between 20th and 21st sts. n. w. This is for the more adult, and the girls are taught a trade.

The Epiphany Church Home is on H. st., between 14th and 15th sts. n. w.

The Home for the Aged is at the corner of 3d and H sts. n. e. It is under the charge of the *Little Sisters of the Poor*. An appropriation of $25,000 was given to the Sisters by Government.

Women's Christian Association, 13th and R. sts. n. w.

HOTELS.

Arlington, on Vermont avenue, near President's House; capacity, 325 guests.

Ebbitt, corner F and 14th sts. n. w.; capacity, 350 guests.

Gray's, corner 15th and I sts. n. w.; on European plan.

Imperial, E st., (facing Penn. avenue,) between 13th and 14th sts. n. w.; $3 per day. Rooms without board. Capacity, 200 guests.

St. James, corner of Penn. ave. and 6th st. n. w.; European plan.

St. Marc., corner of Penn. ave. and 7th st. n. w.; European plan.

Metropolitan, on Penn. avenue, between 6th and 7th sts. n. w.; $3 per day; capacity, 300 guests.

National, on Penn. avenue, corner of 6th st. n. w.; $4 per day; capacity, 500 guests.

Riggs House, corner of 15th and G sts. n. w.

Tremont, corner of 2d st. and Indiana ave., near Balt. and Ohio Depot; $2.50 per day.

Willard's, on Penn. avenue and 14th st. n. w.; terms, $4.50 per day; capacity, 500 guests.

Wormley's, on 15th and H sts. n. w.; $5 per day; capacity, 150.

These are the most notable. There are other hotels of lower prices, suited to all classes of persons.

PLACES OF AMUSEMENT.

National Theatre, on E st., between 13th and 14th sts. n. w. It virtually fronts on Pennsylvania avenue.

Ford's Opera House, on 9th st. n. w., south of Pennsylvania avenue.

Theatre Comique, at the corner of C and 11th sts. n. w.

Avenue Theatre, D st., between 11th and 12th sts. n. w., facing Pennsylvania avenue.

Odd-Fellows' Hall, 7th st., between D and E sts. n. w.

Odd-Fellows' Hall, Navy-yard, Eighth st. s. e.

Masonic Hall, corner F and 9th st. n. w.

Lincoln Hall, corner of D and 9th sts. n. w., in the Young Men's Christian Association Building.

Tallmadge Hall, F st., between 9th and 10th sts. n. w.

Willard Hall, F st., between 14th and 15th sts. n. w.

PRINCIPAL MARKETS.

Centre Market; 410 feet front, between 7th and 9th sts., on the south side of Penn. ave. n. w.; built, 1870.

Eastern Market, on Capitol Hill, at the junction of 7th st. e. and North Carolina ave.; built, 1873.

Western Market, on K, between 20th and 21st sts. n. w.

Northern Market, between 6th and 7th sts. and O and P sts. n. w.; temporarily accommodated in wooden sheds.

Northern Liberty Market, on 5th st., between K and L sts. n. w.; is of brick; 324 feet long; cost $140,000; built 1875.

RAILROADS.

For South, North, East, and West, **Baltimore and Potomac.** Depot corner B and 6th sts. n. w., near Pennsylvania avenue.

For East, North, and West, **Baltimore and Ohio.** Depot corner of C st. and New Jersey avenue, near the Capitol.

HORSE-CAR ROUTES.

Columbia Railway. From the Treasury, 15th st. and New York avenue, to H st. and Boundary n. e. It intersects the Metropolitan at 9th st. and the 7th st. line at 7th st.

Metropolitan Railway. From 17th st., south of Penn. ave., near the State Department, to Senate wing of Capitol.

THE GEORGETOWN AND EAST CAPITOL STREET BRANCH of this route runs from Georgetown, near the Convent, to Lincoln square.

THE NINTH ST. BRANCH, from northern terminus of 9th st. to the Arsenal gate.

SILVER SPRING BRANCH, from northern terminus of 7th st. route to the road leading to Soldiers' Home and Rock Creek Church.

Washington and Georgetown Railway, MAIN BRANCH. At the corner of Pennsylvania avenue and 1st st. n. w. passengers going to or coming from the Baltimore and Ohio depot are transferred without extra charge.

FOURTEENTH ST. BRANCH. From the Treasury, 15th st. and New York avenue, to the Boundary north. Exchange tickets given for Pennsylvania avenue line.

SEVENTH ST. BRANCH. From the Boundary north to the river front. Exchange tickets given for Pennsylvania avenue line.

Capitol, North O st. and South Washington Railroad; or, "The Belt," so called from the circuitous route it traverses. It starts on Maryland avenue, at the foot of Capitol Hill west, south side of the Botanical Garden, and proceeds north to O st., then west to 11th st., then turns south to E st., again west to

14th st., then south to Ohio avenue, which it traverses s. e. to 12th st., then south, crossing the Mall, to Virginia avenue, along which it travels to its intersection with Maryland avenue, then along the line of Maryland avenue to the place from which it started.

These horse-car railroads carry passengers to nearly all the desirable points of interest in the city.

Chariots. There are also lines of chariots, of excellent appointment, going over nearly similar lines of travel.

CHURCHES.

Denominations alphabetically arranged.

Baptist.

FIRST BAPTIST, 13th st., between G and H sts. n. w.

SECOND CHURCH, corner of Virginia avenue and 4th st. s. e.

E-STREET CHURCH, south side of E st., between 6th and 7th sts. n. w.

CALVARY CHURCH, corner of H and 8th sts. n. w.

FIFTH BAPTIST CHURCH, D st., near 4½ st. s. w.

NORTH BAPTIST CHURCH, 14th st., near R st. n. w.

KENDALL MISSION CHAPEL, corner of 13½ and D sts. s. w.

CALVARY MISSION CHAPEL, corner of 5th and P sts. n. w.

METROPOLITAN BAPTIST CHAPEL, (erected 1875,) s. w. corner of A and 6th sts. n. e.

GAY-STREET BAPTIST, corner of Congress and Gay sts., Georgetown.

Baptist Colored Churches.

SECOND BAPTIST, 3d st., near I st. n. w.

THIRD BAPTIST, Franklin, between P and Q sts. n. w.

FOURTH BAPTIST, R st., between 12th and 13th sts. n. w.

FIFTH BAPTIST, Vermont avenue, between Q and R sts. n. w.

SIXTH BAPTIST, corner of 6th and G sts. s. w.

NINETEENTH STREET, corner of 19th and I sts. n. w.

SHILOH, L st., between 16th and 17th sts. n. w.

REHOBOTH, 1st st., near O st. s. w.

MT. ZION, F st., between 3d and 4½ sts. s. w.

LIBERTY CHURCH, E st., corner of 18th n. w.

ABYSSINIAN, Vermont avenue, corner of R st. n. w.

L-STREET BAPTIST, corner of 4th and L sts. n. w.

ENON, corner of 6th st. and South Carolina avenue s. e.

FIRST BAPTIST CHURCH, corner of Dunbarton and Monroe sts., Georgetown.

Christadelphian Synagogue.

CHRISTADELPHIAN SYNAGOGUE, Circuit-Court Room, City Hall.

Christian.

CHRISTIAN CHURCH, Vermont avenue, between N and O sts. n.w.

Congregational.

FIRST CONGREGATIONAL CHURCH, corner of 10th and G sts. n.w.

Episcopal.

ST. JOHN'S CHURCH, corner of 16th and H sts. n. w.

EPIPHANY CHURCH, G st., between 13th and 14th sts. n. w.

TRINITY CHURCH, corner of 3d and C sts. n. w.

CHURCH OF THE ASCENSION, corner of Massachusetts avenue and 12th st. n. w.

CHRIST CHURCH, G st., between 6th and 7th s. e.

GRACE CHURCH, D st., between 8th and 9th s. w.

CHURCH OF THE INCARNATION, corner of 12th and N sts. n. w.

ST. MARK'S CHURCH, 3d st., between A and B sts. s. e.

ST. PAUL'S CHURCH, (Ritualistic,) 23d st. n. w., south of Pennsylvania avenue Circle.

CHURCH OF THE HOLY COMMUNION, 22d st., near E st. n. w.

Lincoln Monument.—(P. 67.)

Ford's Theatre, now Army Medical Museum.

Department of Justice, (Freedman's Bank Building.)

Church of the Holy Cross, corner of 19th and P sts. n. w.

St. Andrew's Mission, 1418 P st. n. w.

St. James' Parish, services in the house, No. 819 H st. n. e.

St. Paul's Church, (Rock Creek,) near Soldiers' Home.

Emanuel Church, Washington st., Uniontown.

Christ Church, corner of Congress and Beall sts., Georgetown.

St. John's Church, corner of 2d and Potomac sts., Georgetown.

Grace Church, High st., between Bridge and Water sts., Georgetown.

St. Alban's, High st. extended, Georgetown.

Episcopal, (colored.)

St. Mary's Chapel, 23d st., between H and I sts.

Friends' Meeting Houses.

Meeting House, (Hicksite,) I st., between 18th and 19th sts. n. w., north side.

Meeting House, (Orthodox,) 13th st., between R and S sts. n. w.

German Reformed Church.

First Reformed Church, corner of 6th and N sts. n. w. German service in the morning; English service in the evening.

Hebrew Synagogues.

Congregation Adas Israel, (Orthodox,) corner of 6th and G sts. n. w. Services every Friday evening at sunset, and every Saturday at 8 A. M. and 4 P. M.

Washington Hebrew Congregation, 8th st., between H and I sts. n. w. Services Friday evening at 7 o'clock and Sabbath (Saturday) morning at 9 o'clock.

Lutheran.

ST. PAUL'S CHURCH, (English,) corner of 11th and H sts. n. w.

MEMORIAL CHURCH, (English,) corner of N and 14th sts. n. w.

GERMAN EVANGELICAL CONGREGATION OF TRINITY, Unaltered Augsburg Confession, corner of 4th and E sts. n. w.

GERMAN EVANGELICAL CHURCH, corner of 20th and G sts. n. w.

GERMAN EVANGELICAL, St. John's Church, 4½ st. s. w.

CAPITOL-HILL MISSION, 1st st., near C st. s. e.

GERMAN EVANGELICAL ASSOCIATION, 6th st., between L and M sts. n. w.

LUTHERAN CHURCH, corner of High and 4th sts., Georgetown.

Methodist Episcopal.

METROPOLITAN, corner of 4½ and C sts. n. w.

FOUNDRY CHURCH, corner of 14th and G sts. n. w.

WESLEY CHAPEL, corner of 5th and F sts. n. w.

MCKENDREE CHURCH, Massachusetts avenue, between 9th and 10th sts. n. w.

RYLAND CHAPEL, corner of 10th and D sts. s. w.

UNION CHAPEL, 20th st., near Pennsylvania avenue n. w.

WAUGH CHAPEL, corner of 3d and A sts. n. e.

HAMLINE CHURCH, corner of 9th and P sts. n. w.

GRACE CHAPEL, corner of 9th and S sts. n. w.

FOURTH-STREET CHURCH, 4th st., between South Carolina avenue and G st. s. e.

TWELFTH-STREET CHURCH, corner of 12th and E sts. s. e.

FLETCHER CHAPEL, corner of New York ave. and 4th st. n. w.

GORSUCH CHAPEL, corner of L and 4½ sts. s. w.

PROVIDENCE CHAPEL, corner of 2d and I sts. n. e.

MT. ZION CHAPEL, corner of 15th and R sts. n. w.

MCKENDREE MISSION, H st., between 8th and 9th sts. n. e.

UNIONTOWN, across the Anacostia, nearly opposite the Navy-yard.

Dunbarton Street, between Congress and High sts., Georgetown.

West Georgetown Church, corner of Fayette and 7th sts., Georgetown.

Methodist Episcopal South.

Mount Vernon Church, corner 9th and K sts. n. w.

Methodist Protestant.

Methodist Protestant Church, on 9th st., between E and F sts. n. w.

First M. P. Church, Virginia avenue, near Navy-yard.

M. P. Mission, corner of 8th st. and North Carolina ave. s. e.

Congress-Street Church, between Bridge and Gay sts., Georgetown.

Mount Pleasant Church, corner of Fayette and High sts., Georgetown.

Methodist Colored Churches.

Wesley Zion, D st., between 2d and 3d sts. s. w.

Union Wesley, 23d, near L st. n. w.

John Wesley, Connecticut avenue, near L st. n. w.

Galbraith Chapel, L st., between 4th and 5th sts. n. w.

Israel Bethel, corner of B and 1st sts. s. w.

Union Bethel, M st., between 15th and 16th sts. n. w.

St. Paul's Chapel, 8th st., between D and E sts. s. w.

Mt. Pisgah Chapel, 10th st., between Q and R. sts. n. w.

Asbury, corner of 11th and K sts. n. w.

Ebenezer, corner of D and 4th sts. s. e.

Asbury Mission, corner Boundary and 9th sts. n. w.

Ebenezer A. M. E. Church, Beall st., between Montgomery and Monroe sts., Georgetown.

Mt. Zion M. E. Church, West st., Georgetown.

A. M. E. Church, Hillsdale, D. C.

A. M. E. Church, Good Hope, D. C.

New Jerusalem.

Temple of the New Jerusalem Church, North Capitol st., between B and C sts. n. e. Seats free.

Presbyterian.

First Presbyterian Church, 4½ st., between Louisiana avenue and C st. n. w.

New York Avenue Church, New York avenue, between 13th and 14th sts. n. w.

Fourth Church, 9th st., between G and H sts. n. w.

Assembly's Church, corner of 5th and I sts. n. w.

Sixth Church, 6th st., near Maryland avenue, s. w.

Western Presbyterian Church, H st., between 19th and 20th sts. n. w., near Pennsylvania avenue.

Metropolitan Presbyterian Church, corner of 4th and B sts. s. e.

Westminster Presbyterian Church, 7th st., between D and E sts. s. w.

North Presbyterian, on N st., between 9th and 10th sts. n.w.

Reformed Presbyterian, 1st st., between N and O sts. s. w.

Central Presbyterian, corner of 3d and I sts. n. w.

Eastern Presbyterian, 8th st., between F and G sts. n. e.

Gurley Mission, Boundary, near 7th st. n. w.

West-Street Presbyterian Church, between Congress and High sts., Georgetown.

Presbyterian, (colored.)

Fifteenth-Street Presbyterian Church, 15th st., between I and K sts. n. w.

Roman Catholic.

St. Patrick's Church, G st., between 9th and 10th sts. n. w. The oldest Roman Catholic Church in Washington.

St. Peter's Church, corner of 2d and C sts. s. e. Built on ground donated by Daniel Carroll, of Duddington, one of the largest original proprietors of the Federal City.

St. Matthew's Church, corner of 15th and H sts. n. w.

St. Mary's Church, (German,) 5th st., near H st. n. w.

St. Dominic's Church, corner of 6th and E sts. s. w.

St. Aloysius Church, corner of North Capitol and I sts n. w.

Church of the Immaculate Conception, corner of 8th and N sts. n. w.

St. Stephen's Church, corner of Pennsylvania avenue and 25th st. n. w.

St. Joseph's Church, (German,) corner of 2d and C sts. n. e.

Trinity Church, corner of 1st and Lingan streets, Georgetown.

Roman Catholic, (colored.)

St. Augustine's Church, 15th st., near L st. n. w.

Unitarian.

Unitarian Church, corner of 6th and D sts. n. w.

Universalist.

Murray Universalist Society, Tallmadge Hall, F st., between 9th and 10th sts. n. w.

Young Men's Christian Association.

Young Men's Christian Association Building, corner of 9th and D sts. n. w. Sunday services at 3½ P. M.

PUBLIC SCHOOLS.

From a recent report of the Commissioner of Education we extract the following information with regard to the Public Schools of the Federal City.

The whole school population of Washington and Georgetown, white and colored, was, in 1873, 29,817. The number of scholars enrolled in the public schools was 14,953. The value of school property amounted to $950,807, the number of buildings owned being 23. Beside these, some other buildings were rented for school purposes.

The colored schools are distinct from the white.

We will mention the locality and names of some of the prominent school-houses :

West of Capitol.

The **Franklin**, at the corner of 13th and K sts. n. w., and opposite one of the most beautiful squares in the city, is an exceedingly fine building of three stories, and contains 14 schoolrooms. (White.)

The **Seaton**, I st., between 2d and 3d sts. n. w.; erected in 1871. The site of this building was, during the late war, occupied by Stanton Hospital. (White.)

The **Jefferson**, corner of 6th and D sts. s. w. This is the largest of all. It was built in 1872, and can accommodate 1200 scholars. (White.)

The **Sumner**, on the n. e. corner of 17th and M sts. n. w.; completed in 1872. This is also a very beautiful building; cost $70,000. (Colored.)

East of Capitol.

The **Wallach**, Pennsylvania avenue, between 7th and 8th sts. s. e.; built in 1864. This was the first great advance in improved public school accommodation in Washington, and received its name in compliment to the then presiding civic dignitary, Mayor Wallach. (White.)

The **Lincoln**, corner of 2d and C sts. s. e. It contains 10 school-rooms, and is a handsome building, with admirable appointments. (Colored.)

WATER-WORKS.

The water supplying the city of Washington is brought from above the Great Falls of the Potomac, 18½ miles from the Navy Yard. The Aqueduct is a succession of wonderful instances of the triumph of the civil engineer. It is a cylindrical conduit of 9 feet internal diameter, and conveys the water from the Great Falls to a *Distributing Reservoir*, 4½ miles from the Capitol. The daily supply is 30 millions of gallons; daily consumption 23 millions, and full capacity of the aqueduct 80 millions of gallons.

The first ground was broken on the Washington aqueduct by President Pierce, Nov. 8, 1853. It has cost three and a half millions of dollars.

Cabin-John Bridge

is one of the distinguishing features of this great enterprise. The bridge is 20 feet wide and 420 feet long; a single arch of 220 ft. spans the chasm. It cost $237,000. Capt., now General Montgomery C. Meigs, of the U. S. Corps of Engineers, was the constructor of this bridge and of the aqueduct.

"The length of pipe line is 18 miles; 12 tunnels, the longest 1,438 feet; total tunnelling, 6,653 feet, and 6 bridges."

FALLS OF THE POTOMAC.

The **Little Falls** of the Potomac are very beautiful, and are about 4 miles above Washington, being a series of cascades in all of 37 feet. It is here the **Chain Bridge**, as it is called, crosses the river. A curious fact is that all the bridges which have crossed the Potomac at this point have been called *chain bridges*, when, in fact, but one was of that construction. The bridge erected here before 1811 was a chain suspension bridge, and its various successors (of which there have been several) have, in turn, been so called. The present one is a Howe-truss iron bridge, *free*, and cost $100,000.

The Great Falls, as already stated, are some 10 miles above the Little Falls, and are wonderfully grand. The rocky channel here is narrowed to 100 yds., and in a series of cascades the river descends 80 feet in the course of a mile and a half. The Virginia shore towers 70 feet of perpendicular rock above the bed of the river.

ANALOSTAN ISLAND

is situated opposite Georgetown, and contains about 70 acres; it is connected with the Virginia shore by a causeway. It was formerly the residence of Gen. John Mason, in the war of 1812 commissary-general. It was once under admirable cultivation, and the earliest known Guide-Book of Washington, by Warden, gives a glowing account of its fertility and the elegant hospitality of its owner. It is now a place of holiday resort for picnics, etc. The mansion still stands, dilapidated and shorn of its former splendor. The Confederate commissioner to Europe, James M. Mason, arrested by Admiral Wilkes, was born on this island.

CEMETERIES.

We have in other places mentioned the Arlington, Congressional, and Oak Hill Cemeteries, and the National Military Cemetery at the Soldiers' Home. There are besides these other cemeteries of interest of considerable extent and beauty lying around the city of Washington.

The oldest of these is Rock-Creek Church Cemetery, near the Soldiers' Home. Rock-Creek Church was first erected in 1719, rebuilt in 1775, and remodelled in 1868. The main walls are those built in 1719. A monument here bears the date of

National Deaf-Mute College.

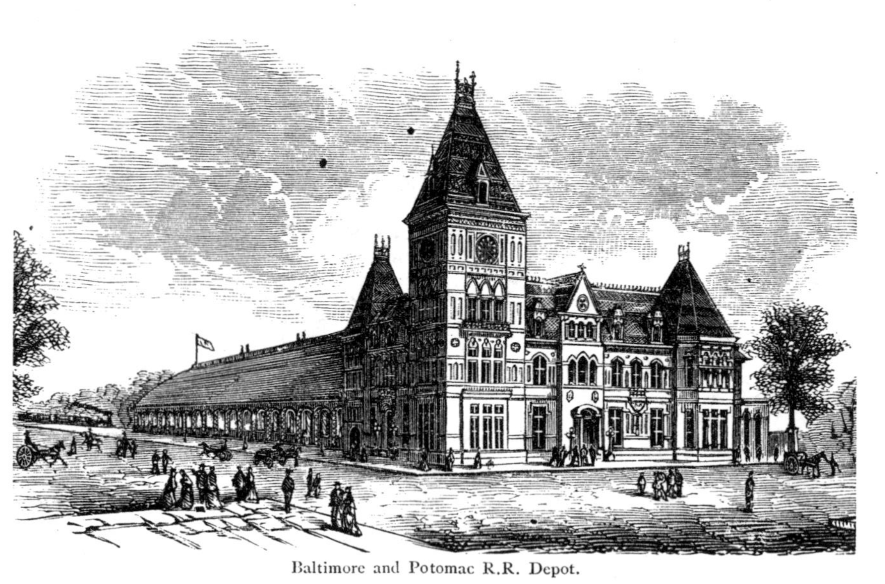

Baltimore and Potomac R.R. Depot.

1775. About one-half of the glebe belonging to this old parish church has of late years been added to the cemetery. The venerable Peter Force, so long conspicuous in the Federal City, is interred here.

Glenwood Cemetery lies about a mile and a half north of the Capitol. It embraces 90 acres, and was incorporated in 1854. Amos Kendall, Postmaster-General in the time of Jackson and Van Buren, is buried here.

Near the entrance to Glenwood are **Prospect Hill Cemetery**, 17 acres; and **St. Mary's Burying Ground**, 3 acres.

Mount Olivet Cemetery, comprising 70 acres, is on the Columbia turnpike, ½ mile north of the east terminus of the Columbia Horse Railway; incorporated in 1862. Many Roman Catholics of eminence are buried here.

Graceland Cemetery, about 40 acres, is situated at the east terminus of the Columbia Horse Railway; opened 1872.

Two of the oldest cemeteries, the Eastern and Western, have been displaced by recent improvements, and the many burying-places immediately surrounding the churches have had for the most part the dead removed from them.

GEORGETOWN

is separated from Washington by Rock creek, and lies northwest of the city. Horse rail-cars enter Georgetown by both the Penn. ave. and P st. routes. It was a town of some importance at the time the Federal City was located. Population in 1870, 11,384.

Georgetown Heights presents admirable building sites, and is occupied by beautiful residences, many of them of a palatial character.

Oak-Hill Cemetery (originally 10 acres) is situated on the Heights, and for beauty of situation, exquisite taste in adornment, and general management, challenges comparison with any cemetery in the world. It has been gradually enlarged, and was originally the gift of Mr. W. W. Corcoran. It now embraces 30 acres.

Secretary Stanton, Chief-Justice Chase, and many other distinguished dead, are buried here.

Georgetown High-service Reservoir, with a capacity of 1,000,000 gallons, is an object of interest. It is at the head of Market st.; the surface water is 215 feet above tide, and 70 feet above the Distributing Reservoir.

The **Convent of the Visitation,** founded in 1799, is an institution of note. In the Convent vault a daughter of Gen. Scott is buried. She was a religieuse of the order. The **Academy** under the care of the Sisters of the Visitation was founded at the same time. In 1873 an addition was made to the establishment. The Academy grounds include 30 acres.

Georgetown College, founded in 1789, raised to an university in 1815, is probably the oldest Roman Catholic college in the country. It is under the care of the Fathers of the Society of Jesus. The library contains many rare works and some valuable manuscripts; and in the MUSEUM are coins and medals, with interesting relics of Commodore Decatur.

The Linthicum Institute and the **Peabody Library** are accommodated in the Public-School building on 2d and Potomac sts.; three stories, basement, and mansard, designed by Adolf Cluss, and cost $70,000; built 1875.

Edward Linthicum, a retired hardware merchant, left by will $50,000 for the education of poor white boys. George Peabody, the world-renowned millionaire philanthropist, (and once a resident of Georgetown,) funded $22,000 to institute the Peabody Library.

A Home for Aged Women is also a thoughtful and beautiful charity of this town.

ALEXANDRIA.

Alexandria is 6 miles distant from Washington. Boats ply every hour during daytime between the two cities, and there is also hourly railroad communication. The city was founded in 1748, then called Bellhaven, the beautiful harbor. Population in 1870, 13,570.

Christ Church is an Episcopal church in Alexandria, over a hundred years old, (1773,) which General Washington used to attend. His pew is pointed out to strangers.

A National Cemetery is near Alexandria, containing the graves of 4,000 soldiers.

MOUNT VERNON,

the home and tomb of Washington, is about sixteen miles down the Potomac from the Federal city. A boat starts daily, excepting on Sunday, from 7th st. wharf, at 10 A. M., for Mount Vernon; returning, it reaches Washington about 4 P. M., thus allowing excursionists ample time to explore the house and grounds.

The scenery between Washington and Mount Vernon is not only beautiful, but replete with interesting national associations. A fine view is obtained of Arlington House, on the Virginia shore. Opposite it is the Washington Monument, forlorn in its unfinished state. Then the receding city passes away like a panoramic view, succeeded by the Arsenal and grounds, the Insane Asylum, and the Navy Yard, while, grandly crowning all, is the Capitol, with its graceful dome.

Alexandria is soon reached. [See Alexandria.]

Fort Foot, an important earthwork during the late war, is next approached. Again the boat stops a moment at old **Fort Washington**. Both forts are on the Maryland shore. The last was built in part by Major L'Enfant. Opposite this fort, on high ground, is Mount Vernon House.

The boat lands at a little wharf reaching far out in the river, belonging to the estate. A walk from this wharf leads to the Tomb.

The front of the vault is open, defended by an open iron gateway, through which the sarcophagus containing the remains of Washington can be plainly seen. There is also another sarcophagus, containing the remains of Martha, the consort of Washington. A number of family graves surround the tomb.

The mansion fronts the river. The centre was built by Lawrence Washington, half-brother of the President, from whom he inherited the estate. The more modern portions were added by the General.

The Mount Vernon Ladies' Association own the mansion and contiguous grounds. Their endeavor is to restore them, as nearly as possible, to the condition they were in during the life of their great owner.

ARLINGTON.

Arlington House is situated on Arlington Heights, in Virginia, on the south side of the Potomac, in plain view of the Capitol. The late war and incidents connected with it have made this a place of historic interest. Over fifteen thousand of the Union dead lie interred around the former beautiful home of the great grand-daughter of Martha Washington, who became the wife of the Confederate chieftain, Gen. Robert E. Lee. The estate embraced about eleven hundred acres, two hundred of which have been set apart as a *National Cemetery*.

A very prevalent mistake, reiterated by irresponsible newspaper correspondents, and copied into several of the Washington Guide-books, it is our duty to correct. It is very positively asserted that in 1863 this estate was "sold under the confiscation act, and in 1864 was taken possession of by the National Government." The facts are that the Arlington property was sold at a *tax sale*, January 11, 1864, and was *never confiscated*. It was never the property of General Lee, and only a *life interest* in the property was devised to Mrs. Lee, by her father, George Washington Parke Custis. The value of the estate, as recorded in the land book of the State, was $34,100. The amount which it was sold for at the tax sale was $26,800. Arlington House was built by Mr. George Washington Parke Custis. It is imposing in appearance, and has a frontage of 140 feet. The portico is 60 feet long and 25 feet deep, and is ornamented with eight Doric columns, built of brick, plastered. It was long regarded as one of the palatial homes of the South. The situation of the mansion is fine, and the view from the portico extensive, and for beauty can scarcely be excelled.

The cemetery lying west of the house is devoted to white and that lying north to colored dead soldiers. South of the house is the "Unknown Tomb," in which are placed the remains of 2,111 unknown soldiers gathered from the battle-fields of Bull Run and the route to the Rappahannock. Near this tomb is an amphitheatre, erected in 1873, designed for use on Decoration Day, capable of accommodating 5,000 persons.

In regard to this estate, it has also been very currently reported that it was bequeathed by Gen. Washington to Mr. Custis, his adopted son. The truth is Mr. Custis inherited it from his father, John Parke Custis, and Gen. Washington never owned it. The founder of the American family of Custis was an emigrant inn-keeper, formerly of Rotterdam, Holland, who, about 1668, married the daughter of Edmund Scarburgh, prominent in early Colonial times as surveyor-general of the State and a representative of Accomac county, Va. The marriage with this lady gave him immense landed possessions.

Fort Whipple,

is situated a short distance northwest from Arlington House. It is the only one of the many forts built near Washington during the late war that has not been dismantled. It is now a station for instruction in signalling.

BLADENSBURG.

This old town, founded in 1750, is in Prince George's county, Md., and is about six miles n. e. of Washington; it is situated on the Anacostia or Eastern Branch of the Potomac, which was in former times navigable to this point, and was the great tobacco centre of the surrounding country.

It is famous for having been, in 1814, the site of the battle of Bladensburg, August 24, in which we were beaten by the British, who pursued the retreating Americans to Washington. The rapidity with which this retreat was effected gained for the unfortunates the facetious title of THE BLADENSBURG RACERS.

Near this village, in a secluded spot, was the famous duelling-ground where Commodore Decatur fell in 1820. Numerous other duels have been fought here, one of the most noted being that in which Graves and Cilley were engaged.

Bladensburg has also been celebrated for a chalybeate spring, claimed to possess medicinal properties of great value.

Proposed Lincoln Monument.

It has been proposed to erect a monument of great elegance and superior workmanship in front of the Capitol to commemorate the history of the Martyr President. An engraving in this volume represents the model, by the artist, Clarke Mills, presented to the committee in charge of the object. Whether it will eventually be placed there remains with the American people to determine. God speed the right!

FOREIGN MINISTERS IN WASHINGTON.

Austria-Hungary.—Count Ladislas Hoyos,* 1021 Connecticut avenue.

Belgium.—M. Maurice Delfosse,* 1714 Pennsylvania avenue.

Brazil.—Councillor A. P. de Carvalho Borges,* 822 Connecticut avenue.

Chili.—Señor Don Adolfo Ibanez,* 1715 H street.

Denmark.—Mr. J. H. de Hegermann-Lindencrone,† 2015 G st.

France.—M. A. Bartholdi,* 1721 H st.

German Empire.—Mr. Kurd von Schlözer,* 734 15th st.

Great Britain.—The Right Hon. Sir Edward Thornton, K. C. B.,* British Legation, Connecticut avenue.

Hayti.—Mr. Stephen Preston,* The Arlington.

Italy.—Baron Albert Blanc,* 2017 G st.

Japan.—Jushie Yoshida Kiyonari,* 926 Scott Place.

Mexico.—Señor Don Ignacio Mariscal,* 1724 I st.

Netherlands.—Mr. de Pestel,† 611 13th st.

Portugal.—Baron de Sant' Anna,* 1725 H st.

Russia.—Mr. Nicolas Shishkin,* 1801 F st.

Spain.—Señor Don Antonio Mantilla de los Rios,* 1301 K st.

Sweden and Norway.—Mr. A. Grip,‡ 2015 G st.

Turkey.—Gregoire Aristarchi Bey,* 1404 H st.

Venezuela.—Señor Don Juan B. Dalla Costa,* Wormley's.

---

* Envoy Extraordinary and Minister Plenipotentiary. † Minister Resident.
‡ Charge d'Affairs *ad. int.*

RATES FOR HACKS AND OTHER VEHICLES.

	Between 5 A. M. and 12.30 A. M.		*Between 12.30 A. M. and 5 A. M.*	
For one or two passengers in a one horse vehicle.	By the hour	75	By the hour	$1 12
	By the trip	75	By the trip	1 12
For one or two passengers, four-seated vehicle, drawn by two horses, within the limits of the city.	By the hour	$1 50	By the hour	2 25
	By the trip, exceeding one mile	1 00	By the trip, exceeding one mile	1 50
For one or two passengers, four-seated vehicle, drawn by two horses, from Washington to or from Georgetown.	By the hour	1 50	By the hour	2 25
	By the trip, exceeding one mile	2 00	By the trip, exceeding one mile	3 00

And for each additional passenger 50 cents. One mile or less, one-half these rates.

In all cases where a vehicle is not engaged by the hour, it shall be considered as being engaged by the trip. It is expressly understood that in all cases the fare for two passengers, together with articles herein provided for to be carried by each, shall be the same as for one only.

The fare to any point outside of Washington and Georgetown, and within the District of Columbia, shall, in all cases, be charged by the hour, or part of an hour, and at the same rate as within these cities, and if the vehicle is dismissed outside of the cities of Washington and Georgetown a fare of fifty cents additional may be charged.

Each passenger is entitled to have conveyed, without extra charge, one trunk, or other travelling-box or bag: *Providing* there be not more than two trunks or other travelling-boxes to be conveyed at one time for the person or persons hiring the conveyance. If there be more than two trunks, the driver shall be entitled to twenty-five cents for each additional one. Each passenger shall also be entitled to have conveyed such other small packages as can be conveniently carried within the vehicle.

The driver shall load and unload all baggage without additional charge.

If a passenger claims to be overcharged by a driver, the driver is compelled to drive the passenger to the nearest police station, where the officer in charge will immediately decide the case. In case where a passenger is about to leave by railroad, stage, or steamboat, the officer on duty at such place shall promptly settle the claim in accordance with law.

www.ingramcontent.com/pod-product-compliance
Lightning Source LLC
LaVergne TN
LVHW021414110826
845150LV00007B/1922

9781425510206